BUILDING FOR THE AGES

OMAHA'S ARCHITECTURAL LANDMARKS

Landmarks, Inc.
Established 1965

KRISTINE GERBER   JEFFREY S. SPENCER

Produced by Omaha Books a division of Eventive Marketing LLC,
P.O. Box 24705, Omaha, Nebraska 68124 (402) 614-0056

First Edition

ISBN 0-9745410-1-X

Printed in the United States of America by Quebecor Books

COVER PHOTOS

TOP ROW (L TO R)
Flatiron Hotel, Joslyn Art Museum, Aquila Court,
Riviera Theater/The Rose

MIDDLE ROW (L TO R)
Masonic Temple/Douglas Building, Otto H. Barmettler Residence,
Riviera Theater/The Rose, Westlawn Mausoleum

BOTTOM ROW (L TO R)
St. Cecilia's Cathedral, Scottish Rite Cathedral,
Rialto Theatre, Old Post Office

PROJECT DIRECTOR
Kristine Gerber

WRITER AND RESEARCHER
Jeffrey S. Spencer

DESIGN
emspace design group

LANDMARKS, INC. COMMITTEE
Ken Mayer, Chair
John Armknecht
Kerry Armknecht
Thomas J. Kohoutek
W. Larry Jacobsen, AIA
J. Robert Perrin, AIA
Annika Phillips
Frank Reida

ADDITIONAL ASSISTANCE
Joanne Ferguson Cavanaugh
Aaron Detter
Jared D. Gerber, AIA
Thomas Heenan
Terry Koopman
Lynn Meyer
Linda Spencer
Stephen Spencer
Dorothy Tuma

INTRODUCTION PHOTOS

(L TO R)
All Saints Episcopal Church, Thomas R. Kimball Residence,
Masonic Temple/Douglas Building, Burlington Station,
Early 16th Street View, Withnell-Barton Residence

Contents

*"When we build let us think that we build forever. Let it not be for present delight
nor for present use alone. Let it be such work as our descendants will thank us for, and
let us think, as we lay stone upon stone, that a time is to come when those stones will be
held sacred because our hands have touched them, and that men will say as they look
upon the labor and wrought substance from them 'See! This our fathers did for us.'"*

JOHN RUSKIN

JOHN RUSKIN, THE FAMOUS 19th century English writer and critic, grasped the immense importance of architecture on shaping the quality environment of future generations. *Building for the Ages – Omaha's Architectural Landmarks,* takes its inspiration from Ruskin's succinct observation. In the timeline of history, Omaha at 150 years is a young city, yet its history is rich and unique, and the quality structures that have stood the test of time are now portals to its future — a future that recognizes design excellence, whether past, present or future, as an essential ingredient to the city's vitality, individuality and sense of pride in what we can become.

This book used 1950 as the cutoff date, omitting structures from the last half of the 20th century. The National Trust for Historical Preservation generally uses 50 years as a criteria for listing on the National Register of Historic Places, and since many of the buildings in this book are either on the National Listing or designated as Landmarks by the City of Omaha's Landmarks Heritage Preservation Commission, we have been consistent in applying that criteria.

While this book focuses on great examples of historical structures that are with us today, we begin by featuring some of the most significant buildings Omaha has lost. We have only photographs by which to experience these icons of our past. We will never be able to tour these buildings, or examine their craftsmanship, or experience the context in which they were situated. They helped shape the quality of Omaha's development, but they are gone forever. Keep this in mind as you view the remaining chapters of the book, for the structures that have survived are the flesh and bones of Omaha's architectural heritage today. They are defining features of our city's image and character — a source of civic pride — and they must continue to play a significant role in Omaha's future.

The buildings have been organized by age groupings beginning with the earliest buildings of Omaha's past and concluding with structures in the 1940s. This offers an opportunity to trace the development and rich diversity of architectural styles and to place the buildings in the context of Omaha's business, social, institutional or political history.

No book of this nature can be totally inclusive. Lack of space meant that many buildings considered for this publication could not be included. Those selected were chosen for architectural significance, contribution to Omaha's unique history, and diverse building types and architectural styles, which help define Omaha's visual tradition.

To the greatest extent possible, we have included current photographs of the buildings. However, several of the buildings are now obscured by landscaping, surrounding walls or other structures. In those instances, we have included historical photographs that present the buildings as they were intended to be viewed, thus providing a full appreciation of the architectural styles and settings of these structures.

Landmarks, Inc. a non-profit organization that serves as an advocate for the preservation of Omaha's historic environment, is proud to sponsor this book. The organization was founded as a result of the controversy surrounding the demolition of the old Post Office building at 16th and Dodge Streets, which stirred preservation advocacy in Omaha.

This book, then, is a celebration of Omaha's architectural landmarks — structures that were built for the ages and have defined the community's character. They testify to the benefits of preservation and provide a glimpse of what this city can become by embracing its past. Community growth can now be balanced with the quality of Omaha's image, recognizing and respecting our unique heritage and architectural legacy.

W. LARRY JACOBSEN, AIA
Past President, Landmarks, Inc.

THE MEANING OF OMAHA has been recorded as "Above All Others on a Stream." The description was derived from the tribal language of the Omaha Indians who lived in the area when settlement began more than 150 years ago.

With the establishment of the Nebraska Territory in 1853 and a treaty of land cession that allowed settlement on the original townsite, Omaha development began in 1854. By the time Omaha was officially incorporated by the Nebraska Territorial Legislature in 1857, the early buildings were already giving way to more permanent structures of brick and stone. Numerous banks and commercial establishments were designed and built creating an atmosphere of growth and optimism.

An economic depression threatened to slow the development of Omaha, but the discovery of gold in Colorado in 1859 provided an impetus for growth. By the close of the Civil War in 1865 and the completion of the Transcontinental railroad in 1869, Omaha was recognized as a key component of Western development.

While the rest of the country suffered financial troubles in the 1870s, Omaha experienced an unparalleled period of growth and change. Architects of local and national acclaim began to transform Omaha from a frontier village to a major city.

Well suited geographically, Omaha soon became an important center of transportation, commerce and manufacturing. The architectural landscape of the city changed as well. The decade between 1880 and 1890 was known as the great "building decade." Omaha saw its original central city transform and develop into the true beginning of city neighborhoods.

During this period, predominately brick structures gave way to imposing commercial edifices of stone, often executed in the Richardson Romanesque style. The creativity and skills of architects were not limited to commissions for commercial buildings. To signify their status and importance in the ever-growing community, prosperous families sought designers for large and elegant mansions, many in the robust Victorian style.

Omaha experienced the difficulties of the great economic depression of 1893. Nevertheless, the business community undertook great civic and community projects. The Omaha Board of Trade promoted business development creating civic groups like the Knights of Ak-Sar-Ben (founded in 1895), which played a prominent role in the city's growth and development. Signs of recovery from the economic downturn in 1895, prompted city leaders to formulate plans to host a World's Fair in Omaha.

The Trans-Mississippi and International Exposition and Indian Congress held during the summer and fall of 1898 centered the attention of the entire world on Omaha. More than 2.5 million visitors came to the exposition grounds between June 1 and October 31.

Business and commercial development remained strong into the first two decades of the 20th century fueled by economic expansion and population increases from European immigrants. New building construction flourished during this period with significant civic, commercial, industrial, institutional, religious and residential structures. This "Golden Age" of Omaha's development was tempered by the continuing challenges of labor, ethnic and political unrest.

After World War I, and through the 1920s and early 1930s Omaha continued to expand in all directions with new neighborhoods, schools and churches. Cultural development blossomed in the downtown area with numerous theaters and the construction of the Joslyn Art Museum. White-collar jobs in the insurance and finance markets began to gain on the predominant industrial, wholesaling and agribusiness markets. The South Omaha livestock industry rose to one of the largest in the country. This period was not without its turbulent times in Omaha's city government. Racial tensions resulted in the 1919 courthouse riot — a black day in the city's history.

The Great Depression, the drought and the dustbowl were hard on Omaha during the 1930s, and while such projects as Union Station and Omaha University were completed during this period, growth slowed considerably. As Omaha began to emerge from the economic morass, war was declared in Europe. War industry activity and jobs brought many people to Omaha during World War II, fueling growth that caused the city to double its size in square miles in the years after the war.

Omaha's postwar boom resulted in a gradual flight from the inner city to the expansive suburbs, first taking the retail businesses from the city's core and then many of the commercial businesses to new office parks surrounding the city. Omaha's

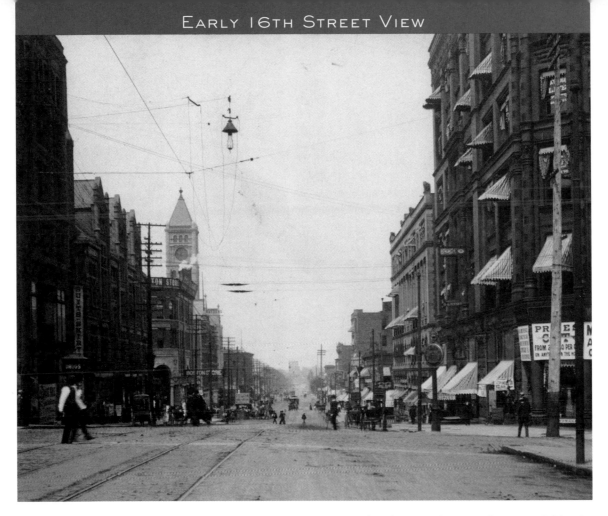

once thriving downtown became a business and government center with little of the attraction it once had as the heart of city life.

Older buildings were under-utilized or vacant. The architecture of the 1960s and 1970s had little appreciation for preservation of the historical environment. Retail, entertainment and hotel businesses were waning in downtown. Racial tensions and riots in the inner city neighborhoods made certain areas of the city unattractive to investors.

Well intended efforts by city and business leaders to redefine the city's core resulted in the demolition of countless historical structures including the old Post Office, Fontenelle Hotel, Woodmen of the World Building, Omaha Athletic Club, Douglas Building and Jobber's Canyon to name only a few. And with each demolition came a growing awareness in the community of the significance of what was lost.

Soon, developers who saw the potential in these structures for adaptive reuse began to invest in their rehabilitation. The Old Market became a benchmark for value in preserving historical structures. By the 1990s, downtown Omaha's resurgence was accompanied by an influx of people moving into the area, almost exclusively in rehabilitated historical structures.

Omaha's first 150 years has seen the waves of significant political, economic and social change. The natives of this area who defined Omaha as "Above All Others on a Stream" were prophetic. Omaha's pride of place and respect for its heritage is well positioned as Omaha takes its place among the great cities in this country.

JEFFREY S. SPENCER

STRUCTURES LOST

When we build let us think that we build forever...

GEORGE W. LININGER settled in Omaha in 1873 and became president of the Lininger and Metcalf Implement Co. His business prospered and he used his wealth to assemble, by far, the finest art collection in the region.

After arriving in Omaha, Lininger purchased a large brick Second Empire mansion at 18th and Davenport Streets. George M. Mills had originally built the house in the late 1860s.

In October 1888, architects Mendelssohn, Fisher and Lawrie were hired to design a large addition that would serve as a gallery for Lininger's fine arts collection. Constructed of brick and terra cotta, it was embellished with belts of gray stone. In an Italian Renaissance style, the most outstanding exterior feature was a row of niches used to display sculpture.

The gallery was 35′ x 70′, with a ceiling 20 feet high. The room was illuminated by an overhead skylight that measured 14′ x 44′. The floor was inlaid tile and marble wainscotting covered the walls. Mahogany and bronze completed the trim elements for a total construction cost of $15,000.

The Liningers opened their gallery regularly allowing the public to view and enjoy the collection.

After Lininger's death, Caroline Lininger continued to live in the home until her passing. At that time the remaining items in the art collection were sold, the house was closed, and then razed in the early 1930s.

18th and Davenport Streets
BUILT: Late 1860s   LOST: 1930s
ARCHITECT: *Unknown*
STYLE: *Italianate/Second Empire*

JOHN NELSON HAYES PATRICK arrived in Omaha in the 1850s from Pennsylvania. An attorney, he accumulated most of his wealth through land speculation and real estate development. Eventually he owned an 800-acre tract of land, west of the city, which he developed into a palatial country estate. He gave it the name Happy Hollow.

In 1871, he constructed a spacious wood-frame house on this site. In 1885, he built an even larger house, and in 1886 joined them together by constructing an immense two-story "great hall" with surrounding exterior porches and roof gables. The total comprised 33 rooms.

Exotic woods were used throughout the interior including walnut, cherry, mahogany and bird's-eye maple. Elegant appointments were evident throughout the home. In time, Patrick possessed one of the finest private collections of American and European paintings in the city, which he used to decorate his home.

In 1888, Patrick established the Patrick Land Co. and began developing Dundee. He also created a private golf course to the west of his mansion.

When he died in 1905 at the age of 77, his heirs sold the large home and adjoining golf course to the newly incorporated Happy Hollow Country Club. The mansion was used as the clubhouse. After the country club relocated, the golf course became the Dundee Golf Club. The house was then sold to Brownell-Talbot School, which took possession in 1923.

The structure was used for several decades, but later was declared unsafe by the Omaha Fire Marshall, and torn down about 1960.

55th Street and Underwood Ave.
BUILT: 1871   LOST: ca. 1960
ARCHITECT: *Unknown*
STYLE: *Eclectic Victorian/Queen Anne*

AFTER THE HERNDON HOUSE at Ninth and Farnam Streets became the headquarters for the new Union Pacific Railroad in 1869, Omaha had no large hotel.

A syndicate was formed and raised $130,000 to construct the Grand Central Hotel. The walls and roof of the five-story structure were completed by the end of December 1870. Then the funds were exhausted and work stopped for almost two years.

The building sat on a limestone foundation, and the basic construction was masonry with load-bearing walls. Limestone lintels and sills were used at the windows. A distinctive mansard roof covered the top.

Another syndicate raised additional capital through a stock subscription and the hotel was finally completed in the fall of 1873. Considered the most elegant hotel in Omaha, its elaborate interior included fireplaces, imported chandeliers and mirrors. The first guests were received in October.

Financial woes surfaced at the beginning. In 1878, a $100,000 mortgage was foreclosed, and on April 18, the property was sold at auction to Augustus Kountze. George Thrall then purchased a lease from Kountze to manage the hotel.

In the summer, the Kitchen Brothers took over this lease and undertook a remodeling and renovation of the hotel. Improvements included the installation of an elevator – a luxury at the time.

On the evening of Sept. 24, 1878, a fire broke out. Before it could be brought under control, five Omaha firemen lost their lives and the hotel was destroyed. A careless workman had left an open candle burning as he left to eat dinner and had caused the fire. In 1882, the first Paxton Hotel was built on this site.

14th and Farnam Streets
BUILT: 1873   LOST: 1878
ARCHITECT: *Unknown*
STYLE: *Italianate/Second Empire*

HERMAN KOUNTZE came to Omaha in the 1850s and soon played an active role in the development of the community. He was the first president of the Omaha Board of Trade, an organizer of the First National Bank, and a founder of the Union Stockyards Co. and the Stockyards National Bank.

In 1878 he built a beautiful mansion on his palatial estate in Park Wild, which he named Forest Hill. It was an elaborate three-story brick structure. Built on a limestone foundation, it had a deep mansard roof covered in slate shingles. There was an ornate covered porch, and the central feature of the house was a four-story square tower.

In 1900, with funds provided by Catherine B. Nash, the property was purchased to create St. Catherine's Hospital. The hospital opened in 1910 and utilized the Kountze house with an attached wing. In 1916, a large three-story addition was made to the existing hospital building.

As further expansion and development became necessary, the original, stately Kountze house was razed in 1924.

Ninth Street and Forest Avenue
BUILT: 1878   LOST: 1924
ARCHITECT: *Alfred R. Dufrene*
STYLE: *Italianate/Second Empire*

GEORGE W. HOLDREGE, general manager of the Chicago, Burlington and Quincy Railroad, played an active and prominent role in the development of Nebraska and the western United States.

After purchasing a large tract of land adjacent to Hanscom Park, he built this imposing wood-frame home.

The house was three full stories. It was built on a limestone foundation and contained a spacious entry hall, 13 rooms and seven fireplaces. All of the interior woodwork was solid oak. One of the first houses in Omaha to be wired for electricity, Holdrege also installed one of the first telephones in the city. A windmill was used to pump water from a well into the house.

The exterior of the house exhibited the exuberant ornamentation of the Queen Anne style and an ornate covered veranda surrounded the main level. There was a large raised gable on the third level that included an open balcony. High brick chimneys rose above the steep, gabled roofline. The property also included a large barn and stable that burned in later years.

In 1910, Holdrege sold the property to John L. Kennedy. Subsequently, Our Lady of Lourdes used the home as a convent for about 40 years. In March 1959 the house was razed and Our Lady of Lourdes school occupies the site today.

2118 S. 32nd Ave.
BUILT: 1883   LOST: 1959
ARCHITECT: *Unknown*
STYLE: *Queen Anne/Shingle*

OMAHA HAD NEED for a public venue capable of accommodating large numbers of people for programs and events. Consequently, a group of Omaha businessmen organized an association to construct an exposition building in April 1885. The south half of a city block between 14th and 15th Streets at Capitol Avenue was leased for a term of 30 years from A. J. Poppleton.

A low brick building, 226′ x 120′ deep, with large square turrets at the corners was erected. The turrets had steeply pitched roofs topped by flagpoles and banners and a series of tall archways and stepped gables surrounded the façade. The initial building proposal specified a construction cost of $25,000; however, this number doubled by completion time. On the evening of Feb. 18, 1886, the hall was formally opened with nearly 5,000 people in attendance.

In the fall of 1886, the Exposition Co. leased an adjoining lot to the north and constructed a 120′ x 66′ addition. The city of Omaha awaiting construction of a new city hall, leased this annex in 1887 to provide temporary space for courtrooms and city offices. When the city vacated that section in 1890, L. M. Crawford leased it and established the Grand Opera House.

The Exposition Co. sold their interest in the combined structure to A. J. Poppleton in February 1891. It continued to be leased for large productions and events until Dec. 4, 1894, when the building was destroyed by fire.

15th and Davenport Streets
BUILT: 1885   LOST: 1894
ARCHITECT: *Unknown*
STYLE: *Eclectic*

THIS IMPOSING STRUCTURE was built as a private residence for Fred Nye in 1887 at a cost of $15,000.

Throughout the years, the home had numerous owners. At one time, it was converted into five apartment units, known as the Roundhouse Apartments.

In November 1944, Grace L. Hill sold the building for $7,000 to the nearby Grace University. It was used as housing for married students attending the school and it was named Bartell Hall in honor of school contributors who had provided funds for its purchase.

The rough-faced exterior stone, the deep heavily arched entry and the integration of a rounded tower into the southeast corner were important Richardson Romanesque features.

The primary construction material was red brick and limestone. Queen Anne elements were exhibited primarily on the second level, by the use of tall chimneys, varied brick patterns, and different window sizes.

The interior had undergone extensive modifications, and little is known of the original appearance.

The building was condemned by the city when it was found to be in dangerously deteriorating condition. Interior fixtures were sold at auction, and in January 1980, the structure was razed.

1502 S. 10th St.
BUILT: 1887   LOST: 1980
ARCHITECT: *Hodgson and Sons*
STYLE: *Richardson Romanesque/Queen Anne*

ONE OF THE MOST UNIQUE HOMES IN OMAHA, both in style and history, began as a rather small, simple farmhouse of wood construction. Henry and Mary Meyers built it on their land at 24th and Pratt Streets in the mid-1870s.

This property was purchased about 1885 by real estate developer and entrepreneur Clifton E. Mayne. He used the profits from his Orchard Hill development to enlarge and reconstruct the Meyers farmhouse.

When completed, his spectacular Victorian mansion contained 20 rooms. A five-story central tower with covered balcony at the top, soared to a height of 60 feet. A wide, circular covered veranda surrounded the entire first floor. The first floor featured an immense parlor, dining room and spacious entry hall. An elegant porte-cochere was attached to the side. Numerous decorative chimneys rose high above the gabled and turreted roofline. The interior of the frame house was completed with exotic woodwork and fixtures.

Mayne experienced numerous financial difficulties and, in 1889, went to San Francisco. Attorney John I. Redick purchased the house from Mayne's creditors.

By 1907, Oak C. Redick, heir of John I. Redick, sold the house for $30,000 to the newly organized Municipal University of Omaha although funds could not be raised until 1909.

The structure, known as Redick Hall, became the first home of Omaha University, now known as the University of Nebraska at Omaha.

With the development of the campus, the house was inadequate, and in 1917 it was sold to Rudolf Beal, an Omaha grain dealer, who with his family owned a resort at Currie, Minnesota. He dismantled the house and shipped it by rail car to Keeley Island on Lake Shetek. There it was rebuilt and became the Valhalla Dance Pavilion and Cafe until a fire destroyed the building March 3, 1928.

3612 N. 24th St.
BUILT: ca. 1875   LOST: 1917
ARCHITECT: *Unknown*
STYLE: *Flamboyant Queen Anne*

FRANK MURPHY, an early Omaha banker and business leader, had this imposing house built for him in 1889. Murphy, president of the Merchant's National Bank, as well as president of the Omaha Street Railway Co., had arrived in Nebraska Territory in 1857.

Situated on a corner lot, the structure was an amalgamation of two purely American architectural approaches; Romanesque style, in the H.H. Richardson form, and Shingle style. A raised basement and the first floor were constructed in red sandstone and the upper stories were clad with rounded shingles. The moderately pitched hipped roof, with broad based gables, and dormers with polygonal and convex roofs, produced an effect that was much quieter than the also popular Queen Anne style.

A raised covered front entry porch, Romanesque and prominent, dominated the main façade. A low retaining wall, also in red sandstone, elevated the lot from the street, and a large stable and carriage house were located to the north along the alley.

Frank Murphy passed away in New York in 1904. His sister, Mrs. Thomas B. Cuming (widow of Nebraska's second Territorial Governor), resided at the house until 1915. A succession of Mrs. Cuming's family members, and then tenants, which included a maternity hospital and a medical fraternity, culminated in the sale of the property in 1945. The house was promptly demolished and the site is currently home to a tanning parlor.

2204 St. Mary's Ave.
BUILT: 1889 LOST: 1945
ARCHITECT: *Unknown*
STYLE: *Richardson Romanesque/Shingle*

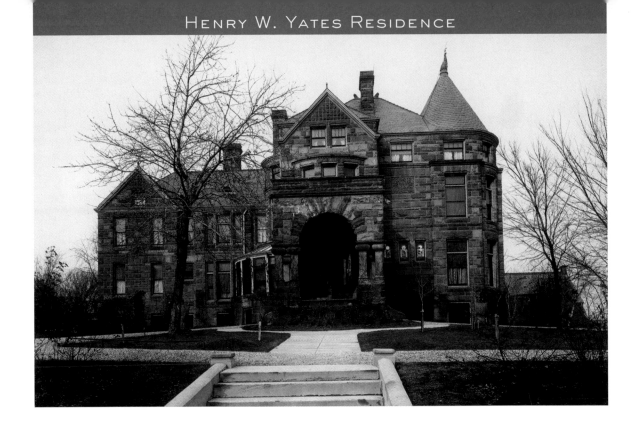

HILLSIDE WAS THE ESTATE OF HENRY WHITEFIELD YATES SR., president of the Nebraska National Bank. Constructed of irregular blocks of buff Amherst stone, it was three full stories and contained 30 rooms. Building began in 1887 and took two years to complete. The initial cost was $40,000. The firm of Rice and Bassett, from Austin, Illinois, was the contractor and Herts and Co. of New York provided all of the interior decorations.

The overall plan was asymmetrical, with a large rounded wall tower on the east. Numerous chimneys and gables rose above the steeply pitched slate roof.

A central feature of the interior was a large entry hall (20′ x 40′) with a 12-foot ceiling. The hall, which included the front staircase, was finished in heavily paneled quartersawn oak. An enormous carved stone fireplace extended to the ceiling. The rooms were elegant with inlayed parquet floors. The dining room was finished in solid mahogany with a large fireplace and beamed ceiling. Most magnificent was the drawing room, decorated in pink and gold, with painted frescos on the ceiling and gold plated lighting fixtures. A conservatory and library were also located on the main floor. There were 10 bedrooms and six bathrooms.

In 1915, after the death of Yates, the family sold the west half of the property for construction of Yates Elementary School.

Mrs. Yates continued to live in the home until her passing in 1929. The house was then rented to the Bickel Advertising School. Thereafter, a medical fraternity rented until 1943. In 1944 the land was sold and the house razed. The Hillside Court apartments occupy the site today.

3120 Davenport St.
BUILT: 1889   LOST: 1944
ARCHITECT: *F. M. Ellis*
STYLE: *Eclectic/Richardson Romanesque*

AS EARLY AS 1880, Omaha needed an adequate City Hall. In 1882, voters approved the acquisition of a site on the northeast corner of 18th and Farnam Streets.

In 1889, an architectural design competition was offered. Omaha architect Charles F. Beindorf from the firm of Fowler and Beindorf submitted the winning design. The construction contract was awarded to John F. Coots from Detroit, Michigan who had built the nearby Douglas County Courthouse.

Work progressed so that on June 19, 1890, the cornerstone was laid. A large crowd attended, including eight former Omaha mayors, and the Masonic Grand Lodge of Nebraska set the stone.

When completed, the total cost was approximately $550,000. The raised basement and first level were built of granite and levels two through five were red sandstone. An elaborate flight of marble steps led from the main entrance into an atrium court. On the southwest corner of the structure, a tower rose nearly 200 feet.

The interior was even more lavish. All of the interior woodwork was solid oak. The main council chamber held an enormous ornate brass chandelier. The ceiling frescos and wall murals were painted by Gustave Fuchs. Later, a sixth floor was completed on top of the building, and in 1915 "bird cage" elevators were installed in the open court.

Early on, construction flaws appeared, especially in the tower. In 1919, Mayor James C. Dahlman required the top section of the tower be removed.

Remodeling was done in 1950, which greatly altered the original façade. The steeples and gables were removed, flattening the roofline. But in 1962, the Public Safety Director officially classified the structure as dangerous. It continued to be used however, until it was sold in 1966 and in March of that year it was demolished. The Woodmen Tower now occupies the site.

18th and Farnam Streets
BUILT: 1890   LOST: 1966
ARCHITECT: *Fowler and Beindorf*
STYLE: *Romanesque/Gothic Revival*

As OMAHA GREW, the public water supply was a frequent topic of concern. In 1878, the city began planning for an adequate system. In 1881, the City Waterworks Co. began construction on a workable system. Their successors, American Waterworks Co., opened a large and improved pumping station eight years later. At the time of its construction, this station was the finest facility of its type in the country.

The Minne Lusa (Florence) Pumping Station was constructed entirely of Warrensburg sandstone. It had a large, square central tower that rose to a height of five stories. The main entrance was a massive rounded stone archway. Many of the exterior stone blocks exhibited a rusticated finish.

The interior contained huge, high volume steam powered water pumps. Large coal-fired boilers provided steam power. There was an elaborate water filtering system. The structure was 120′ x 160′, and entirely illuminated by electric lights.

The basic structure was three stories high. More than 200 men labored for two years on its construction. A great public opening celebration was held Aug. 1, 1889.

Between 1968 and 1970, the main superstructure of the pumping station was taken down, and a remodeled building was placed over the original foundation and equipment.

9100 N. 30th St.
BUILT: 1889   LOST: 1970
ARCHITECT: *Mendelssohn, Fisher & Lawrie*
STYLE: *Richardson Romanesque*

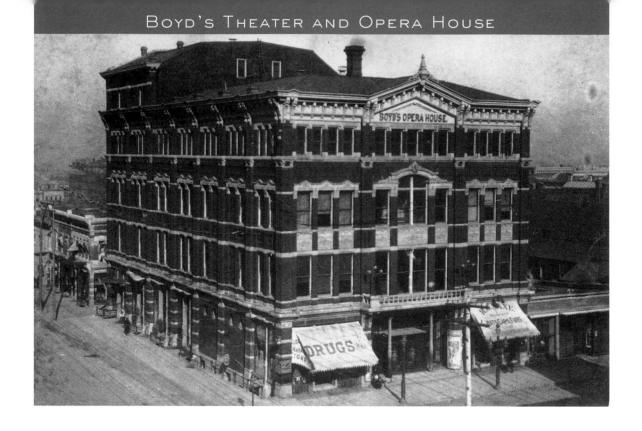

BOYD'S THEATER AND OPERA HOUSE

JAMES E. BOYD was a prominent figure in the development of Nebraska and Omaha. He served as Nebraska's governor and as Omaha's mayor. Upon his arrival in 1856, he was involved with railroad building, real estate development and meat packing, and played a significant role in the development of South Omaha.

In 1881, he first built Boyd's Opera House at 15th and Farnam Streets. After this structure burned, he built a new theater and opera house at 17th and Harney Streets.

This five-story structure was built and furnished for $250,000. It opened to the public Sept. 3, 1891. Constructed on an iron frame, the exterior was pressed brick. There was commercial space on the street level, as well as office space within.

The main auditorium provided seating for 2,000. The greatest entertainers of the day appeared on the stage including Sarah Bernhardt who performed "La Tosca" in 1905.

Governor Boyd died in 1906. The theater was sold to the Burgess-Nash Co. in 1914. They continued to manage it as a theater until 1920, when the theater was razed to provide space for an annex to the Burgess-Nash Department store.

1621 Harney St.
BUILT: 1891   BUILT: 1920
ARCHITECT: *Unknown*
STYLE: *Commercial/Classic Revival*

In 1886, the First Methodist Episcopal Church purchased two lots at 20th and Davenport Streets for $9,000. Fund-raising projects were undertaken and construction began in April 1889 with R. Stevens and Sons acting as general contractors.

The architects designed a magnificent building, 80′ x 89′. The walls above the limestone foundation were of Portage red sandstone and Roman pressed brick. The façade incorporated decorative patterns of brickwork and terra cotta ornamentation and the overall design was a cruciform pattern, with a street level entrance on all sides.

A central feature was the square bell tower that rose 130 feet. It was 20 feet square at the base, and had three large cast copper gargoyles at the top.

The interior contained a huge pipe organ and an auditorium that would seat 1,200. All woodwork was red oak and the floor of the impressive vestibule was covered with brown and buff colored glazed tile. The church was among the first in Omaha to be wired for electricity.

A dedication service of the partially completed structure was held on Sunday, June 8, 1890.

On Jan. 11, 1954, the building was destroyed by fire. The congregation, now known as First United Methodist Church, built a new church at 69th and Cass Streets where they are located today.

20th and Davenport Streets
BUILT: 1891   LOST: 1954
ARCHITECT: *Mendelssohn, Fisher & Lawrie*
STYLE: *Modified Romanesque Revival/Spanish Gothic*

WITHNELL/BARTON RESIDENCE

THIS LARGE THREE-STORY HOME was originally built for John Withnell Sr., president of Withnell and Smith, a construction and brick manufacturing company. Red brick construction and extensive use of red sandstone ornamentation gave mass to a design configuration, which was irregular and interesting. The southwest corner of the main façade contained a large rounded tower, tasteful and restrained.

In contrast to the somewhat sedate exterior, the interior rooms were finished with many costly and elegant appointments. After Guy C. Barton purchased the house in 1902, he redecorated the music room and called it the Gold Room. The style was Louis XV, with frescos, gilt ornamentation and mirrors. A crystal chandelier hung from the center of the room, and the walls were covered in silk tapestry. Throughout the house, solid cherry, mahogany and walnut were used for woodwork.

At the rear of the property a large carriage house provided living space and was well appointed. It contained a trophy room and a large stable finished in glazed tile.

In 1914 after the death of Mr. and Mrs. Barton, the home was sold to H.S. Clarke, an Omaha banker. Clarke sold it to the Heafey family who converted the home to Heafey and Heafey Mortuary in 1928. It remained in this use until 1980, when the property was sold to Security National Bank. The carriage house was razed in September 1981 and finally the main residence in June 1982.

3522 Farnam St.
BUILT: 1892   LOST: 1982
ARCHITECT: *Fisher and Lawrie*
STYLE: *Romanesque Revival/Queen Anne*

FROM THE BEGINNING IN 1884, the Omaha Club was considered the most prestigious private club in Omaha. In any given year, its membership roster was a who's who of the city's most influential citizens.

As membership increased, a new clubhouse on the northwest corner of 20th and Douglas Streets was built. Its cornerstone was laid in 1893, and the structure was completed in January 1895. With three stories plus a full basement, the building was constructed of light granite, buff brick and terra cotta trim. Construction cost was $100,000.

The 20th Street anciliary entrance formed an arcade of three arches. At third level, a recessed balcony was set into the main

façade. The interior had an "air of quiet elegance." A beautiful and imposing hall mantle was finished in embossed tile with carved seats at either end.

The design for the club was executed by Charles F. Beindorf, a young architect who was born in Omaha in 1864. He had previously won the competition for the design of the Omaha City Hall in 1889. After his work on the Omaha Club, he designed the Horticulture Building for the Trans-Mississippi and International Exposition in 1898. Tragically, his promising career ended with his death in October 1898.

The Omaha Club building was demolished in November 1965, to make way for a more modern facility.

2002 Douglas St.
BUILT: 1895 LOST: 1965
ARCHITECT: *Charles F. Beindorf*
STYLE: *Italian Renaissance Revival*

As PRESIDENT OF THE CUDAHY PACKING Co. in South Omaha, E. A. Cudahy was one of the most prominent and wealthy businessmen in Omaha. He commissioned Chicago architect Henry Ives Cobb (1859 - 1931) to design this Late Gothic Revival home. Cobb was especially well-known for his designs of the University of Chicago and later commercial buildings in New York City.

In size and quality of materials, this was one of the most significant residential structures ever built in Omaha. Containing 22 spacious rooms, it was three full stories and had 10 fireplaces and seven bathrooms. Of load-bearing masonry, the house was constructed in gray brick with carved Bedford limestone trim and detailing.

Sharp, high gables rose above a steeply pitched roof that featured large dormer windows. The driveway curved from 37th Street through large iron gates to a porte-cochere that was ornamented with Gothic arches. More than 5,000 pounds of copper were used for downspouts and roof trim.

The interior detailing was spectacular as well. The ceilings on the first floor were 11 feet high. Those on the second floor were 10 feet, and the third floor ceilings were nine feet. The main floor exhibited ornate, solid mahogany woodwork, with hand-carved representations of musical instruments. Three magnificent stained glass windows lit the stairwell landing.

A large carriage house provided additional living space for servants and a massive limestone wall surrounded the entire property.

Cudahy had purchased the site in 1894, and the house was completed in 1897. Before moving to Chicago in 1912, the Cudahy family sold the home to Fred A. Nash. Nash sold the home to Dr. Henry A. Schultz, who was the last owner. The house was razed Feb. 9, 1964, to make way for a luxury apartment building.

504 S. 37th St.
BUILT: 1897   LOST: 1964
ARCHITECT: *Henry Ives Cobb*
STYLE: *Late Gothic Revival*

EDWARD WATROUS NASH AND CATHERINE BARBEAU NASH arrived in Omaha from Canada in 1868. They had recently married, and were seeking a future in the developing west. In time, Nash became president of the American Smelting and Refining Co., and a prominent member of the local business community. In the 1880s, in partnership with Guy C. Barton, he made a fortune from silver mines in Mexico. Part of those proceeds was used to purchase a two-acre tract of land on the northwest corner of 38th and Burt Streets. Here he built his large, ornate residence. A large barn with a high lantern cupola and stable were also on the property.

The two and one-half story home was constructed in wood and a highly ornamental covered porch surrounded the exterior of the first level. The central feature of the house was a three-story rounded tower, capped by a high cupola with a circular balcony on the second level. The interior was finished in exotic solid hardwoods, that included mahogany, cherry and bird's-eye maple.

After the death of E. W. Nash in July 1905, Mrs. Nash continued to reside in the home until her passing in 1928. In the early 1930s, the property was sold and the lot divided. In January 1933, the Chambers Wrecking Co. razed the house and salvaged the beautiful interior woodwork for resale.

3806 Burt St.
BUILT: ca. 1887   LOST: 1933
ARCHITECT: *Unknown*
STYLE: *Victorian/Queen Anne Revival*

WHEN A REFERENCE IS MADE to a lost architectural landmark in Omaha, it is the old Post Office that is most often remembered. Almost no other single structure symbolized the architectural heritage of our community as did the old Post Office.

During the period of Omaha's youth, the Post Office occupied various rented locations. In 1874 a fine structure was completed on the southwest corner of 15th and Dodge Streets. In time, it was outgrown and a larger facility was needed.

In 1889 a Federal appropriations bill in the amount of $1.2 million allowed funds for site acquisition and the construction of a new Post Office. Located at 16th Street, between Dodge Street and Capitol Avenue, the government provided plans, and Omaha architect Charles F. Beindorf was initially appointed the onsite supervising architect. On his death, John Latenser Sr. assumed that position. Work on the foundation began in 1892, by O. J. King, the building contractor. In time, a truly imposing and monumental building in the Richardson Romanesque style took shape.

The basement and first story were a rough textured St. Cloud pink granite. Above this were three levels constructed of sandstone. The main entrance faced east toward 16th Street and was approached through a loggia, 15-feet wide and 50-feet long, surmounted by a balustrade. Five large rounded arches rising from massive piers, defined this entrance. The arches were embellished on each side by polished granite columns and carved capitals. Over the center of the loggia rose a square tower that achieved a height of 190 feet, complete with a large clock face on each of the four sides.

Prominent gables with triple window groups denoted the Dodge Street and Capitol Avenue entrances. With a roof of copper panels, the structure was built around an open atrium court. Ceilings on the interior of the first level were 22 feet high and a skylight 100 feet square covered the courtyard.

Although a formal opening was held Feb. 22, 1898, the building was not entirely completed until 1906. Total cost when finished was $2 million.

Due allegedly to the costs of repair and maintenance the General Services Administration of the Federal Government declared the building surplus and built a new facility in the early 1960s.

Although there were many suggested plans to redevelop this landmark, none materialized. The site was acquired by the First National Bank, and in the summer of 1966 the Post Office building was demolished. A bank office building and a hotel replaced it.

As a result of public concern and awareness associated with the fate of the Post Office, Landmarks, Inc. was organized in 1965.

16th and Dodge Streets
BUILT: 1898 LOST: 1966
ARCHITECT: *U.S. Government*
STYLE: *Richardson Romanesque*

WITH A STRATEGIC CENTRAL LOCATION and close proximity to major railroad lines, Omaha became an important wholesale distribution or "jobbing" center in the 1880s. From 1900 to 1918 over 20 brick warehouses were built in a six-block area, located to the east of downtown Omaha. The name Jobbers Canyon was given to the area due to the canyon-like space formed along either side of Ninth Street.

Plain, utilitarian structures in form, with limited use of ornamentation, the designs emphasized the functional nature of the buildings. Many of them had special fire safety innovations, which were of great importance at that time.

Important structures included:

THE NASH BLOCK - 902 Farnam St.

Designed by Thomas R. Kimball, and built between 1905-1907. Two large eight-story structures were leased to the M. E. Smith Co.

THE KINGMAN IMPLEMENT CO. - 923 Farnam St.

Designed by Charles Cleves, and built in 1900, with additions in 1905 and 1916. A large six-story building.

FAIRBANKS-MORSE AND CO. - 902 Harney St.

Designed by Fisher and Lawrie, and built in 1907. Distinguished by a very prominent entry arch, the building had six stories.

JOHN DEERE PLOW CO. BUILDING - 402 S. 9th St.

Designed by O. A. Eckerman of Moline, Illinois, in association with Fisher and Lawrie in Omaha. Built in 1908, with eight stories, it was the largest structure in the district.

CARPENTER PAPER CO. BUILDING - 815 Harney St.

Designed by John Latenser Sr. and built in 1906, with an addition in 1928. Eight stories high, it displayed distinctive limestone trim on the exterior of the first two levels.

CREIGHTON BLOCK - 824 Howard St.

Designed by Charles Cleves and built in 1905, the building was eight stories. It housed the large Byrne-Hammer Dry Goods Co.

OMAHA COLD STORAGE CO. BUILDING - 809 Farnam St.

Designed by Fisher and Lawrie and built in 1913. This immense Prairie style building had 10 stories; six built initially in 1913 and four more added in 1919. It served the wholesale grocery trade.

With changing needs in the community, many of the buildings were vacated. In the mid-1980s plans emerged for the redevelopment of the Omaha riverfront area, and did not include these buildings. After some delay, demolition began in 1988. In total, 16 major structures were razed.

Eighth to 10th Sts; Farnam to Jackson Sts
BUILT: 1900s   LOST: 1988
ARCHITECTS: *Numerous*
STYLE: *Primarily Renaissance Revival/Commercial*

ARCHITECT THOMAS R. KIMBALL designed this home for his brother, Richard R. Kimball, on property adjacent the original Kimball family home on Park Wild Avenue. Richard R. Kimball was a prominent early automobile dealer in Omaha, as well as a founder of the Omaha Country Club. He also managed farm and ranch land belonging to the Kimball family.

This house was one of the earliest local examples of the Georgian Revival style that became very popular in the following two decades. It was built of red brick, with load-bearing masonry construction.

The two and one-half story house had a prominent central roof dormer that contained a decorative arched Palladian window. An ornamental wood railing enclosed the crest of the roof. Limestone was used for the exterior trim.

Tuscan columns supported a substantial front porch, topped by a high balustrade. A large two-story porch was located at the rear of the house where the lot sloped steeply to the east.

In 1914, the house, as well as the original T. L. Kimball residence next door, was given by the Kimball family to the Creche, a day nursery for working mothers that was founded by Mary Rogers Kimball.

The property was sold by the Creche in 1928 and subsequent owners razed the house in the mid-1960s.

1235 Park Wild Ave.
BUILT: 1901   LOST: mid-1960s
ARCHITECT: *Thomas R. Kimball*
STYLE: *Georgian Revival*

At the turn of the 20th century, South Omaha was a rapidly growing community. With an increasing need for community facilities, the Andrew Carnegie Library Fund made available a grant of $50,000 to build and equip a public library.

The City of South Omaha purchased a lot at 23rd and M Streets in 1902, for $3,500, as a site for the new library. Prominent Omaha architect Thomas R. Kimball created the design, reminiscent of a small Italian Renaissance palazzo.

The building was two stories over a fully raised basement level. The main floor was devoted to library services, while the second floor contained a large assembly room.

The central feature of the main façade was a heavy rounded arch over the entrance. Two symmetrical sidelights and two large arched windows flanked the entrance.

The construction was brick and rusticated limestone, capped by a modestly pitched red clay tile roof. Solid oak woodwork was used throughout the interior. When South Omaha was annexed to the City of Omaha in 1915, this library became the first branch of the Omaha Public Library system.

This building was razed in December 1953 and a new library was constructed in the same location and opened in October 1954.

23rd and M Streets
BUILT: 1904   LOST: 1953
ARCHITECT: *Thomas R. Kimball*
STYLE: *Renaissance Revival*

ONE OF THE MIDWEST'S MOST GIFTED Eclectic Era architects, Thomas R. Kimball drew plans for his own home in 1902. Work did not begin until 1905, at which time he also supervised construction of his mother's house just a block away.

In this design, Kimball drew on a full spectrum of architectural tradition, and the result embodied Colonial Revival, Tudor, and Jacobethan elements. The house was constructed in solid masonry and featured a side gabled slate roof with stepped parapeted walls. The main façade included a circular entry porch with four Corinthian columns and upper balustrade. On third floor appeared three steeply pitched gable dormers with carved vergeboards. The north and east elevations featured two

octagonal tower-like projections; one was three stories, and contained the circular staircase, and the other was a larger two-story element that housed the octagonal dining room on the first floor and a bedroom on second floor. The seven-fireplace house had three stories, each constructed on two levels, and gave visitors the sense of a six-level home.

Kimball completed his plan by designing a curved drive and elaborate gardens, the whole surrounded by decorative masonry walls with iron fence, all on a corner lot.

By 1937, both Mr. and Mrs. Kimball had passed away. The house was razed in 1940 to make way for a grocery store and parking lot.

2450 St. Mary's Ave.
BUILT: 1905   LOST: 1940
ARCHITECT: *Thomas R. Kimball*
STYLE: *Eclectic*

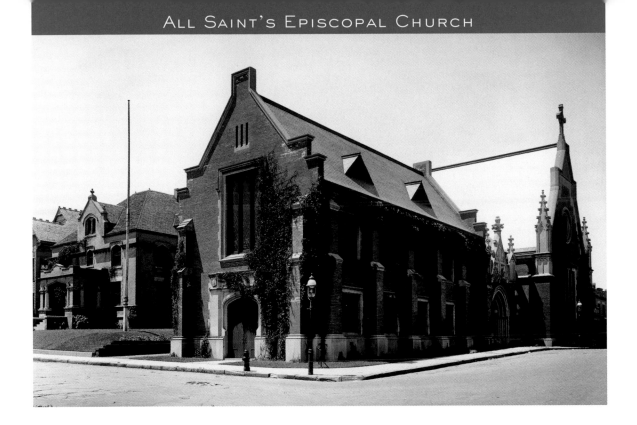

THE PARISH OF ALL SAINT'S was organized in the spring of 1885. In October of 1887, a wood frame church was completed at 26th Street and Dewey Avenue. By the turn of the 20th century, the needs of the congregation had outgrown the small building and plans were undertaken to build a new and larger church and a parish house.

In 1904, a new rectory designed by John McDonald was built to replace the first one damaged by fire. Soon after, the church itself was damaged by a storm, precipitating an acceleration of the building plan. Architect Thomas R. Kimball designed both buildings and construction began in the spring of 1906.

The new church and parish house were constructed at right angles to each other. A covered entry connected them and a carriage drive at the rear provided easy access to both.

The church had a simple nave, with seating for 480 persons. It was 125′ x 48′, and rose 70 feet high at the apex of the roof. Built of red brick, with a gray slate shingle roof, the main entrance was deeply recessed, and overhead was a large plaque of carved limestone with a cross in bas-relief.

The cost of the church was $50,000, and the adjoining parish house cost an additional $15,000. The completed parish house and church buildings were dedicated on Easter Sunday 1907.

In November 1933, a fire severely damaged the church. In the 1960s the congregation moved to a northwest location and the property was then sold. The building was razed in 1966.

26th Street and Dewey Avenue
BUILT: 1906   LOST: 1966
ARCHITECT: *Thomas R. Kimball*
STYLE: *Modified Gothic Revival*

IN 1901 THOMAS R. KIMBALL drew plans for this home for Winifred Agnes Gallagher, widow of Ben Gallagher, founder of the Paxton and Gallagher Wholesale Grocery Co. Construction commenced in 1902 and Mrs. Gallagher occupied the grand house in 1904.

Numerous classical design elements of the Eclectic Era were combined to produce a structure that greatly characterized the substantial Gold Coast neighborhood. Constructed of solid masonry and finished in gray Omaha pressed brick, the three-story over raised basement home was trimmed extensively with Bedford limestone. The main façade was perfectly symmetrical, and featured an elaborate covered entry porch with 10 limestone columns that supported cornice and balustrade. Typical of Kimball's work were the varying window treatments given to each of three floors. At the third level, flush dormers pierce the roofline and accent the steeply pitched slate covered roof. Offset multi-story demilune projections were prominent design features on the north and south façades and added great interest to the exterior, as well as the interior, floor plan.

A slightly elevated lot at street-side was retained by a low brick and limestone wall with pillars at both the front entrance and the carriage entry.

No less elaborate than the exterior, the interior featured a center hall design and included fine hardwoods, wall coverings of silk and other fabrics, and numerous fireplaces.

Throughout its history the Gallagher family occupied the home. Mrs. Gallagher died in 1920 and her son Paul Gallagher and his family were in residence until his passing in 1966. Creighton University received the property as a gift and then sold it to a developer. The house was demolished in 1967 to construct an apartment building in its place.

513 S. 38th St.
BUILT: 1904   LOST: 1967
ARCHITECTS: *Thomas R. Kimball*
STYLE: *Classical Revival/Eclectic*

THE HOTEL FONTENELLE was the result of an ambitious building project undertaken by the Douglas Hotel Co. and its president, Gurdon W. Wattles. The concept, to build a $1 million hotel, became reality when Arthur Brandeis and John L. Kennedy donated one-quarter block of land on 18th and Douglas Streets, valued at $200,000.

In 1913, architect Thomas R. Kimball was commissioned to create the design and supervise construction. In addition, he also provided designs for many of the interior elements, such as fixtures and furniture. The new hotel was named for Logan Fontenelle, a leader of the Omaha Indian tribe.

The central feature of the façade was an ornate "crown" of terra cotta spires, intended to symbolize an Indian headdress. They were, more properly, a Venetian style. The remainder of the façade was quite plain, yet substantial.

The interior featured many costly appointments and amenities. Guestrooms were finished in English décor, and each room was equipped with a telephone. The main lobby was paneled in mahogany and the large dining rooms had richly decorated walls and beamed ceilings. Floors were covered in marble and tile. The main banquet room could seat 500, and had five crystal chandeliers.

Originally, the hotel contained 15 stories (later expanded to 18) and had 350 rooms. The structure was 154' x 131' at the base. Above the fourth level it assumed a "U" shape. The main entrance was located on Douglas Street, with a secondary entrance on 18th Street. Both had large canopies extending over the sidewalk.

Construction material was reinforced concrete, in the "post and beam system." Exterior walls were clay tile faced with dark brown brick. All floors and the roof were reinforced concrete. The roof sheathing was fabricated with interlocking sheets of copper.

The Fontenelle Hotel opened to great fanfare Feb. 15, 1915. Financial difficulties caused the lessee, the Nebraska Hotel Co., to fail in 1920. The next year, the hotel was taken over by Eugene C. Eppley who operated the hotel until he sold it to the Sheraton Hotel Co. Closed, Feb. 28, 1971, the Fontenelle Hotel remained vacant for a number of years. After the failure of several redevelopment plans, the building was razed in the spring of 1983.

1806 Douglas St.
BUILT: 1914   LOST: 1983
ARCHITECT: *Thomas R. Kimball*
STYLE: *Late Gothic Revival*

THE WOODMEN OF THE WORLD LIFE INSURANCE CO. was the largest fraternal life insurance company in the world when they initiated construction of an 18-story building in 1911.

Chicago architects, Holabird and Roche, designed the building and local architects, Fisher and Lawrie, supervised construction. The Seldin-Breck Co. of St. Louis, Missouri were the contractors.

Costing approximately $1.5 million when completed, it was the tallest building between Chicago and the Pacific Coast. The dedication ceremony occurred on Oct. 3, 1912.

The exterior had a pink granite base under white terra cotta and red brick. It was "L" shaped, and built on a steel frame. Concealed electric lights in the decorative cornices lighted the exterior at night with dramatic effect. The elegant lobby featured an impressive white marble staircase topped by four large bronze Egyptian Revival urns. Decorative bronze grills covered the six elevators, and the main entrance on Farnam Street contained a motor driven revolving door.

In 1919, a 19th floor was added to accommodate one of the first broadcasting stations in the country, WOAW later known as WOW.

In 1927, Woodmen of the World sold the building but leased office space there until 1934 when they relocated to the Insurance Building. The old Woodmen of the World building was razed in 1978.

1323 Farnam St.
BUILT: 1912   LOST: 1978
ARCHITECT: *Holabird and Roche*
STYLE: *Classical Revival/Commercial*

THIS BEAUTIFUL THEATER was built primarily as a movie theater to seat 2,500. The contractor was Calvin Ziegler, and it was constructed for the Blank Realty Co. Cost of construction was $125,000. The theater was built on a steel frame, with concrete and masonry walls. Terra cotta was used for exterior trim and detailing.

As the theater had a small triangular stage, it was not well-suited for vaudeville performances. With a large three-manual 30-rank Hillgren-Lane concert organ, it opened to the public on Memorial Day, 1918. During the next decade the theater was adapted to talking pictures.

Closing suddenly Aug. 2, 1929, the Rialto was divided into several retail establishments, and subsequently used as a bus station, a bowling alley, a retail-clothing store and a cafeteria. The large organ was acquired by Central High School with a plan to install it in the school auditorium. Never accomplished, the organ was dismantled and sold for scrap.

The building was razed in February 1986 to be replaced by a parking lot and is today the site of Union Pacific's new headquarters building.

1424 Douglas St.
BUILT: 1918   LOST: 1986
ARCHITECT: *John Latenser and Sons*
STYLE: *Classical/Georgian Revival*

THE OMAHA ATHLETIC CLUB was a notion of George Brandeis and A. P. Hansen. They had visited clubs in other cities and wished to bring the concept to Omaha. Arthur Brandeis sold the men a prime location lot at a greatly reduced price as his contribution to the new enterprise. It was Arthur Brandeis's last business transaction before he died.

The 10-story structure, designed by the Latenser firm, was built by the Selden-Breck Co. at a cost of $400,000.

The first two stories were faced with Bedford limestone, and the upper stories were artistic red brick with stone trim. An ornate portal, with an adjustable automatic canopy, flanked by bronze torchlights, extended over the sidewalk.

The interior was magnificent. Club members enjoyed unlimited use of the dining room, lounges, bowling alley, fourth-floor swimming pool, gymnasium, and comfortably furnished rooms for out-of-town guests. This was all topped by a roof garden, where Freddie Ebener's orchestra played for weekend dances. The Omaha Athletic Club, the scene of major social and business activity, closed in 1970.

The property was sold in 1977 for possible redevelopment; resold in 1983, and razed in 1992. This is now the site of the Roman L. Hruska Federal Courthouse.

1714 Douglas St.
BUILT: 1918 LOST: 1992
ARCHITECT: *John Latenser and Sons*
STYLE: *Neoclassical Revival*

SINCE 1877, NUMEROUS MASONIC LODGES and related Masonic organizations shared Freemasons Hall at the corner of 16th Street and Capitol Avenue. Membership in these organizations flourished during the early years of the 20th century, and the site at 19th and Douglas Streets was purchased to construct a new and larger facility.

Omaha architect George B. Prinz, designed this building and an elaborate cornerstone laying ceremony was held Oct. 4, 1916. More than 5,000 people were in attendance with a grand parade on Douglas Street.

Primary construction material was limestone and brick. The ground floor, designed for retail use, featured large windows, various entrances, and smooth and rusticated stone. The middle stories were buff-colored brick, with sets of windows alternated with engaged pilasters topped with carved Corinthian capitals.

The building contained 105,000 feet of space, distributed through seven stories. It was designed along the then popular concept of the Chicago School "divided pillar" façade treatment of base, shaft and capitol. The structure was enhanced by an exuberance of detailing and a variety of stone finishes. The pronounced cornice, topped by a slightly coved attic story, gave the building a distinctive character.

At one time, the building held eight Masonic Lodges, as well as the Grand Lodge of Nebraska and the Grand chapter of the Eastern Star. Commercial tenants occupied the first level and the second and third floors were used for Masonic offices and kitchens. The fourth and fifth levels contained elaborate meeting and lodge rooms. The sixth floor featured a large auditorium with a mezzanine balcony. The top floor housed mechanical facilities.

The Masonic Temple Craft of Omaha continued to utilize the building until it was sold in 1981. At that time, the name changed to the Douglas Building.

This substantial structure was razed in 1997 to make way for a small parking lot to adjoin the new Roman L. Hruska Federal Courthouse.

19th and Douglas Streets
BUILT: 1918   LOST: 1997
ARCHITECT: *George B. Prinz*
STYLE: *Classical Revival/Beaux Arts*

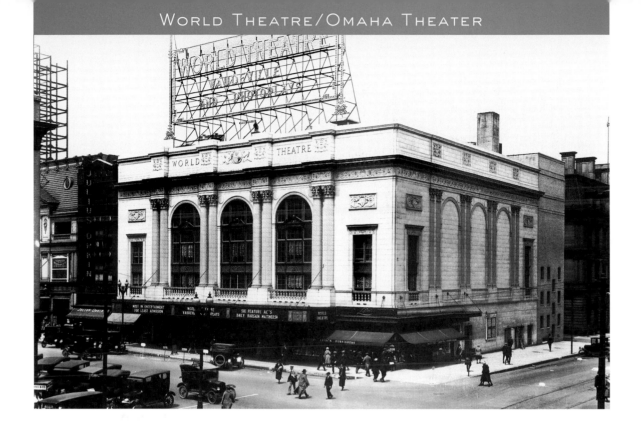

NOTED DETROIT ARCHITECT, C. HOWARD CRANE initiated the design of this structure for the World Realty Co. Crane was one of the foremost theatrical architects in America. Architect Harry Lawrie supervised the project in Omaha.

The theater was constructed on a steel framework with brick walls. The entire surface of the main façade was covered in glazed terra cotta, exhibiting much detail and classical ornamentation. The James Black Masonry and Construction Co. carried out the 10-month construction project. Decorative columns were used on the exterior, as well as several ornamental friezes.

The interior of the vaudeville and silent movie house was no less spectacular. It included a large three-manual 10-rank Wurlitzer organ and seated 2,100 patrons. The theater opened April 15, 1922.

In February 1935, under new ownership, the name was changed to the Omaha Theater. It continued operation until closing Feb. 26, 1978.

When plans for redevelopment could not be realized, the theater was razed in 1980 to make way for a city parking garage.

1506 Douglas St.
BUILT: 1922   LOST: 1980
ARCHITECT:
C. Howard Crane/Harry Lawrie
STYLE: Greco-Roman Revival

CONCEIVED BY OMAHA PHYSICIAN Dr. W. P. Wherry, as a modern rendition of an all-purpose medical office and laboratory facility, the newly formed Medical Building Construction Co. Association obtained the site in 1919. They commissioned architect Thomas R. Kimball to develop a comprehensive design. The plans were completed and construction began in 1920.

Almost from the beginning, the project experienced financial difficulties. After only the structural steel framework was complete, the building association went bankrupt. Due to non-payment of his fees, architect Kimball withdrew – taking all of the construction plans with him.

Construction was suspended for three years before the frame was sold to a syndicate of Chicago investors. This company issued bonds to raise capital and the needed funds to continue building.

A local architect, Joseph G. MacArthur, was engaged to assist W. Crosby of Chicago, to move forward. This proved difficult. The builders then turned to John and Alan McDonald to supervise the project. The McDonald's had a working relationship with Kimball, and obtained necessary plans and specifications to finish the building. This was done in 1926 for a total cost of $2 million.

When completed, the Medical Arts Building was 17 stories high finished in decorative brick with terra cotta and limestone trim. The terra cotta ornamentation was especially interesting.

The first floor held six commercial spaces, each having a street level entrance. An auditorium seating 500 was located on the second floor. Office floors were hard maple, the public corridors terrazzo. Marble wainscot covered the hallway walls to a height of seven feet. A tearoom was placed on the top 17th floor.

Additional financial difficulties ensued in May 1931, when the Chicago syndicate defaulted on the construction bonds. The U. S. National Bank promptly foreclosed and later sold the building to the Connecticut General Life Insurance Co. in 1947. Held by Connecticut General until 1961, it resold to a local group organized as the Medical Arts Building Co. At a loss, they sold the building in 1968 to the Fidelity Corporation of Richmond, Virginia, the last major owner.

The building was demolished April 2, 1999, to make way for the new First National Bank. The limestone Tudor-Gothic cornice of the building was salvaged and installed in the Winter Garden of the First National Bank Building.

17th and Dodge Streets
BUILT: 1926   LOST: 1999
ARCHITECT: *Thomas R. Kimball*
STYLE: *Classical/Beaux Art*

OMAHA BUILDING
· MDCCCLXXXVIII ·

New York Life Building

PRE-1900

Let it not be for present delight nor for present use alone...

BANK OF FLORENCE

Designated Omaha Landmark: Oct. 14, 1980   *Listed on the National Register of Historic Places*

THIS BUILDING, constructed in 1856, is the oldest existing structure in Omaha.

First chartered by the Nebraska Territorial Legislature in January 1856, the bank building was constructed later that year for the firm of Cook, Sargent and Parker, who came to the new town of Florence from Davenport, Iowa. Levi Harsh built the building for $4,500.

The brick used in construction was brought up the Missouri River from St. Louis. The vault was made from large plates of sheet steel from Pennsylvania. Although the overall style is quite simple, it is defined by a heavy cornice and balanced door and window placement. The exterior remains almost totally original. The interior has been extensively remodeled, although the original vault remains in place.

With the Panic of 1857, this bank failed, as did all others in the area. Later, the building was utilized for various purposes, including a stable. In 1904, the Bank of Florence was re-chartered, and the interior renovated for commercial use.

Presently, the structure is owned by the Florence Historical Foundation, has been partially restored, and is used as a museum.

8502 N. 30th St.
BUILT: 1856
ARCHITECT: *Unknown*
STYLE: *Greek Revival*

THIS BUILDING IS ONE OF THE OLDEST structures in Omaha and was originally built for the wholesale grocery firm of Steele, Johnson and Co. The original three-story structure features a cast iron storefront that surrounds the windows and door of the first floor. This allowed for the placement of large display windows at street level. Construction is red brick, with limited use of limestone trim. Sometime between 1882 and 1884, a fourth floor was added, and a decorative metal cornice was installed at the roofline.

In 1887 Daniel Baum located in Omaha and with his two sons established the Baum Iron Co. The business expanded greatly. In 1916 the Omaha Iron Store Co. merged with the Baum Iron Co. and the combined businesses became known as the Omaha Baum Iron Store Co.

The Baum Iron Co. continues in operation today, and the handsome façade of this building remains unaltered thus pleasing many passersby.

1221 Harney St.
BUILT: 1871
ARCHITECT: *Unknown*
STYLE: *Italianate/Commercial*

Listed on the National Register of Historic Places as part of a Historic District

THE OLD MARKET HISTORIC DISTRICT, located east of the central business district, played an important role in the early development of Omaha as a wholesale jobbing center. Initially a residential site in the 1860s and 1870s, the area gave way to developers such as Dr. Samuel D. Mercer, Frederick L. Ames and Andrew J. Poppleton, as they sought to fulfill the needs of many merchants and businesses for storefront and warehouse space. Soon, the entire area became an important distribution and jobbing center for a host of goods and merchandise shipped by Union Pacific Railroad to all parts of the expanding west.

Most of the structures were built with load-bearing masonry walls and the designs were provided by many of Omaha's leading architects. Today the buildings that served the 19th and 20th century food brokers, commission merchants, printers and the producers and distributors of light manufactured goods, are home to a variety of restaurants, shops and loft apartments.

The Old Market is a vibrant area, considerably enhanced by the diversity of architectural styles and designs, and is a popular tourist destination in the state of Nebraska.

HARNEY TO HOWARD: 10th to 13th Streets
HOWARD TO JACKSON: 10th to 12th Streets
BUILT: 1880 to 1905
ARCHITECTS: *Numerous*

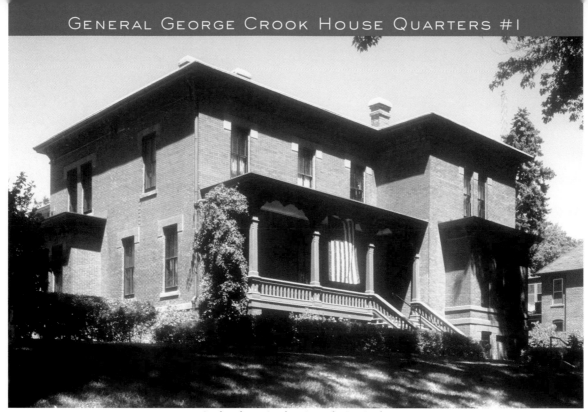

Listed on the National Register of Historic Places

AN 1878 U. S. ARMY REGULATION specified that all officers would live on post. As a result, a Post Commander's residence was constructed at Fort Omaha in 1879. Referred to later as the Crook House, the structure was designed by George Field, a U.S. government architect. The resulting large two-story house is constructed of brick, with sparse limestone trim, following the popular Italianate style of the time. Construction cost was $7,716. The plan is asymmetrical, with a hipped roof, two large open porches and a window bay.

The first occupant of the house was General George Crook who was stationed in Omaha as Commander of the U.S. Army's Department of the Platte. He served in that office from 1875 to 1882, and again from 1886 to 1888. The house is named for him.

In 1905, the structure was used as a bachelor officer's club and mess hall. It was converted back to the post commander's residence in 1930, remaining as such through final closing of Fort Omaha in 1973. Later, the house was acquired through a lease agreement from Metropolitan Community College to serve as offices, exhibit space and a house museum for the Douglas County Historical Society. The Society has restored the house, both exterior and interior, with much care and attention to detail.

Fort Omaha
30th and Fort Streets
BUILT: 1879
ARCHITECT: *George Field*
STYLE: *Italianate*

Listed on the National Register of Historic Places as part of a Historic District

FIRST ESTABLISHED as a military post in the 1860s, the name officially became Fort Omaha in 1878. At that time, the new fort also officially became the headquarters for the Department of the Platte.

This two and one-half story headquarters building is one of the first permanent structures built at Fort Omaha. It is brick masonry construction, with limestone windowsills and arches. Several one-story wood porches, executed in the Eastlake design, are distinctive features.

This structure was used as a departmental headquarters office for a relatively short time during the tenure of General George Crook. Later, his office was moved to a downtown Omaha location, nearer to rail and supply outlets.

The U. S. Army declared the fort surplus property in 1947 and the area then became a Naval Reserve Manpower Center. It was again declared surplus and closed permanently in 1973. At that time, Fort Omaha became the campus of Metropolitan Technical Community College.

Today, Fort Omaha continues to serve as the north campus of Metropolitan Community College. The headquarters building has been extensively remodeled on the interior and is utilized as the campus library.

In keeping with lease covenants, the historic façade of the structure has been preserved and maintained.

Fort Omaha Campus; 30th and Fort Streets
BUILT: 1879
ARCHITECT: *U.S. Government*
STYLE: *Italianate Revival*

BURLINGTON HEADQUARTERS BUILDING

Designated Omaha Landmark: Oct. 17, 1978 *Listed on the National Register of Historic Places*

THIS STRUCTURE, originally a three-story building, was built as the local headquarters for the Burlington and Missouri, later the Chicago Burlington and Quincy Railroad.

It is brick with load-bearing masonry walls on a foundation of limestone blocks.

The simple design features a flat roof, straight front and sides, with a minimal use of limestone trim. A heavy ornamental cornice at the roofline ties the design together.

In 1886, a fourth story was added to provide more office space. Cast iron columns, rather than load bearing walls, support the floor marking a transition in building techniques.

Architect Thomas R. Kimball was commissioned to direct a remodeling of the building in 1899. The interior was totally redesigned to resemble the great Chicago, Burlington and Quincy Railroad Co. building in Chicago.

A central atrium with skylight, accents the second through fourth floors. A decorative, open staircase was installed with galleries overlooking the enclosed courtyard. An elevator was placed at the southeast corner. Fenestration opening toward the court is set off by dark colored brick, while the wall surfaces are covered in a lighter glazed brick. Woodwork is quartersawn oak.

The building was occupied by the railroad until 1966. After standing vacant for a time, it was renovated in 1982 for use as office space. The renovation was completed in a sensitive and historically accurate manner.

1002–1006 Farnam St.
BUILT: 1879
ARCHITECT: *Alfred R. Dufrene/*
Thomas R. Kimball
STYLE: *Italianate*

BROATCH BUILDING

Designated Omaha Landmark: Dec. 20, 1983   *Listed on the National Register of Historic Places*

LOCATED IN OMAHA'S OLD MARKET DISTRICT, the first section of the Broatch Building was constructed in 1880 as a three-story building by William J. Broatch. Broatch was Omaha's first heavy hardware wholesaler, establishing his business in 1874.

The building was designed to serve as both an office and warehouse and was enlarged in 1887 to its present four stories and 20,000 square feet. Broatch maintained his business there for 40 years.

In 1979, the architectural firm of Bahr, Vermeer and Haecker purchased the building and completely renovated the structure for use as their office and other commercial space.

The historic integrity of the original exterior has been well maintained including the distinctive cast iron façade on the ground floor.

1209 Harney St.
BUILT: 1880
ARCHITECT: *Mendelssohn & Lawrie*
(1887 addition)
STYLE: *Italianate/Commercial*

Designated Omaha Landmark: July 13, 1982   *Listed on the National Register of Historic Places*

THIS STRUCTURE IS A FINE EXAMPLE of commercial buildings designed in the Italianate style and typical of the form used prior to the 20th Century. The three story brick building was built by Andrew Jackson Poppleton, an early pioneer of Omaha, for whom Poppleton Avenue is named. Poppleton was a prominent local attorney and served as General Attorney for the Union Pacific Railroad.

Although Poppleton financed the construction of the building, still in use today, he never occupied the offices.

1001 Farnam St.
BUILT: 1880
ARCHITECT: *Henry Voss*
STYLE: *Italianate/Commercial*

ORIGINALLY CONSTRUCTED AS WAREHOUSES for wholesale food distribution, Ray Ford later purchased these buildings to serve as a distribution center for neighborhood markets in Omaha.

When Ford entered the moving and storage business, the structures were converted. Ford's was the first moving company in Omaha to use gasoline-powered trucks.

The buildings were very substantial and well built and have remained in good condition over the years.

In the late 1990s, NuStyle Development Corp. completed a renovation of the buildings creating 186 residential units with retail bays along Jones Street.

Building #14
1007 Jones St.
BUILT: 1881
ARCHITECT: *Unknown*
STYLE: *Italianate Revival/Commercial*

Building #13
1009 Jones St.
BUILT: 1886
ARCHITECT: *Unknown*
STYLE: *Classic Revival/Commercial*

Building #12
1019 Jones St.
BUILT: 1918
ARCHITECT: *John Latenser Sr.*
STYLE: *Commercial*

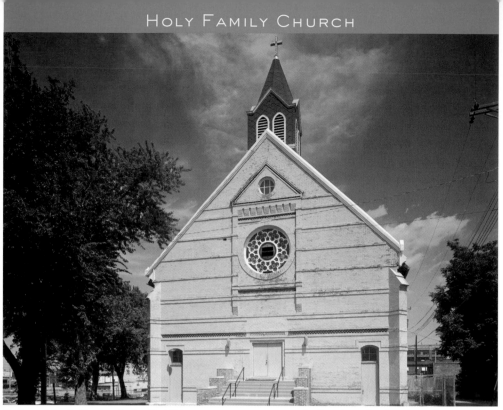

Designated Omaha Landmark: Oct. 22, 1985　　　*Listed on the National Register of Historic Places*

HOLY FAMILY CHURCH is the oldest existing Catholic Church building in Omaha. It is also the earliest known commission executed by the Cleves brothers.

The church structure was built in 1883, to incorporate a church, school and a rectory. It was intended to serve the increasing Irish immigrant population that worked for the nearby Union Pacific Railroad.

Constructed of brick, it combines elements of both Gothic and Romanesque revival styles. However, as it was built in the midst of the Victorian period, it is a mixture of many distinctive stylistic elements. Built on a simple rectangular shape, it had classrooms in the basement and living quarters for the clergy at the rear.

The basic structure retains most of its original design features, and the façade is unchanged. It continues in use as a parish church today.

915 N. 18th St.
BUILT: 1883
ARCHITECTS: *Charles and August Cleves*
STYLE: *Gothic Revival/Romanesque Revival*

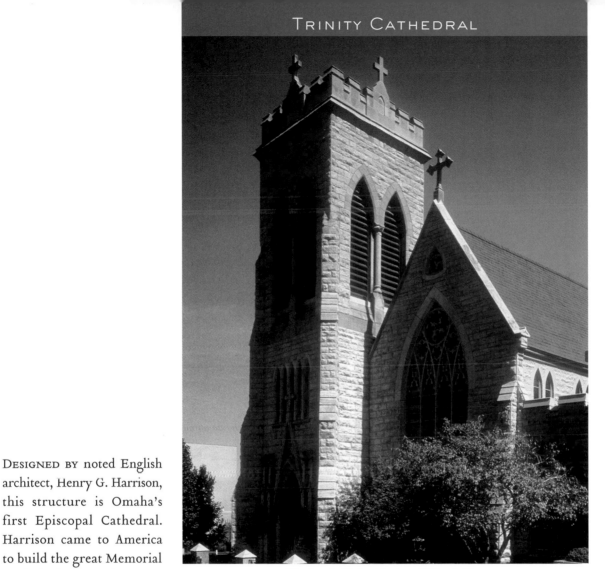

Listed on the National Register of Historic Places

DESIGNED BY noted English architect, Henry G. Harrison, this structure is Omaha's first Episcopal Cathedral. Harrison came to America to build the great Memorial Cathedral in Garden City, Long Island, New York.

Two local architects, Alfred R. Dufrene and A. T. Large, supervised the construction. Ground was broken for the Cathedral May 15, 1880, and it was consecrated Nov. 15, 1883.

Built almost entirely of blue Illinois limestone, the design is nearly cruciform with an added tower extending outward, which also serves as an entrance. The tower can be seen from the street in both directions. Smooth dressed stones outline the doors, windows and gable. Several crosses are atop the building.

The decorative interior includes 43 stained glass windows. Thirteen of these entirely surround the apse depicting Christ and the Apostles.

There are many gothic features in the interior design and the carved oak bishop's throne and dean's stall are especially noteworthy.

Throughout the long history of this church, there have been very few alterations.

113 N. 18th St.
BUILT: 1883
ARCHITECT: *Henry G. Harrison*
STYLE: *Late Gothic Revival*

Designated Omaha Landmark: Jan. 6, 1981   *Listed on the National Register of Historic Places*

CHRISTIAN SPECHT, a native of Berlin, moved from Cincinnati to Omaha in 1880. Here, he established the Western Cornice Works, manufacturers of galvanized iron cornices, metal dormer windows, finials, window caps, tin and iron roofing and a specially designed metal skylight which Specht invented and patented.

This distinctive building features the finest existing cast metal façade in Omaha. Cast iron fronts were mass-produced with ornate detailing and could be put up quickly. However, as cast metal could not accommodate wide expanses, buildings like this had a rather narrow frontage.

Behind the cast metal front, the three-story building is constructed of Omaha pressed brick, with wood panel floors and joists. It has a characteristic high first level, with large windows.

The building was originally used as a commercial warehouse. The interior room arrangement allowed for an open floor plan and there was a staircase at the rear.

Specht owned the building for a fairly short time, and it has had numerous owners since. Today, it serves as both commercial and residential space and is in very good condition.

1110 Douglas St.
BUILT: 1884
ARCHITECT: *Dufrene and Mendelssohn*
STYLE: *Italian Renaissance Revival*

DR. SAMUEL D. MERCER RESIDENCE

Listed on the National Register of Historic Places

DR. SAMUEL D. MERCER came to Omaha in the capacity of chief surgeon for the Union Pacific Railroad. He later developed professional connections with the University of Nebraska Medical Department, the United States Pension Examiners, and the Nebraska Medical Association. Dr. Mercer was the founder of Omaha's first hospital.

Between 1883 and 1885, he constructed a 23-room red brick residence at 40th and Cuming Streets. His mansion reportedly cost $60,000 and features a three-story square tower that rises above the south side main entrance.

The structure exhibits many decorative forms popular in the Victorian era including various colors and textures, as well as relief panels of brick and terra cotta. Stained glass windows and hallway transoms were utilized throughout the house. Interior detailing included the extensive use of decorative hardwoods, arched doorways, carved woodwork and parquet floors.

Much of the elaborate Victorian wood trim, including a distinctive Eastlake design porch across the front of the house, was removed in 1926. At that time, a wing was added to the west side of the house and the ornate stable at the back of the property was demolished and replaced with automobile garages.

The Mercer family was in residence until 1920, at which time the house was divided into apartments.

3920 Cuming St.
BUILT: 1885
ARCHITECT: *Unknown*
STYLE: *Queen Anne Revival*

JOEL N. CORNISH RESIDENCE

Listed on the National Register of Historic Places

THIS ELEGANT MANSION is one of the earliest great homes still standing in Omaha. Joel N. Cornish built it in 1886, the year he moved to the city. Cornish, a lawyer and businessman, later served as president of the National Bank of Commerce.

The house is constructed of red brick with a slate roof and decorative detail rendered in wood on the exterior. Standing three stories, the house contains 15 rooms with four marble fireplaces and originally had a ballroom on the third floor. The main floor originally had 13-foot ceilings and carved walnut woodwork with bands of decorative parquet inlay surrounding the hardwood floors.

An apartment wing was attached to the back of the house in 1911. The house remained in the Cornish family until it was sold in 1956. In 1958, it was acquired by Grace University and converted into apartments. Many of the high ceilings were lowered at that time and the interior has undergone some changes, but the exterior remains unchanged despite the removal of some decorative elements.

Distinctive near, or from afar, the Cornish house is the best example of its style in the city.

1404 S. 10th St.
BUILT: 1886
ARCHITECT: *Unknown*
STYLE: *French Second Empire*

BEMIS OMAHA BAG CO. BUILDING

Listed on the National Register of Historic Places

THIS LARGE FIVE STORY STRUCTURE occupies almost one half of a city block and was constructed in three phases, between 1887 and 1902.

Constructed by Harte and Lindsay, it is Omaha's earliest example of a simplified commercial style architecture which was developed in Chicago. The structure housed the Bemis Co., manufacturer and distributor of cloth and paper bags and sacks used for flour, grain and other products.

The Bemis Omaha Bag Co. ceased operation at this location in March 1978. In 1983, the building was sold to the Mercer family and converted to living spaces for the Bemis Project, a not-for-profit artist colony. After a time, the Bemis Project and the artists relocated to the nearby McCord-Brady building. In 1999 a fire damaged the original section of the Bemis Bag building. It is now used for residential and commercial space.

614 – 624 S. 11th St.
BUILT: 1887
ARCHITECT: *Mendelssohn and Lawrie*
STYLE: *Commercial Style*

Designated Omaha Landmark: Jan. 6, 1981

THE CORNERSTONE for St. John's was laid June 26, 1887, before a gathering of 4,000 people. The event attracted so much attention that late in the evening thieves attempted to steal the copper box contained within the cornerstone!

P. J. Creedon of Creedon and Berlinghof was the architect for this, the second building constructed on the campus of Creighton University. He designed the church in the English Gothic style and utilized Warrensburg sandstone for the exterior. The main part of the church was completed in 1888, but it did not include the transept and apse due to a lack of funds.

In 1922, Omaha architect Jacob M. Nachtigall was engaged to supervise the resumption of construction. By 1927, all was complete except the right tower.

The family of John A. Creighton provided many of the interior furnishings. The high altar cost $5,600 and was the gift of John A. McShane, a Creighton nephew. Mrs. Creighton donated one of the windows and the furniture for the sanctuary. Following her death, Creighton donated the Stations of the Cross in her memory. Other parish members gave the organ and additional appointments.

In 1977, the steeple was finally added to the right tower. When this work was completed, the structure manifested the original design first set down 90 years before in 1887.

2500 California St.
BUILT: 1887
ARCHITECT: *Patrick J. Creedon, Jacob Nachtigall*
STYLE: *Gothic Revival*

Listed on the National Register of Historic Places

THIS DISTINCTIVE STRUCTURE is all that remains of Krug Brewery's complex of buildings. Originally, the numerous buildings comprised the largest brewery operating in Omaha. This structure is constructed of load-bearing red brick, which exhibits a decorative pattern. Notable are the rounded, arched, window and door openings, and the corbelled brick articulation of the walls. The front third of the building served as an office, the two large bays on the east side were used for a reception area and executive offices, and the large space at the rear for storage and barrel making.

When the Krug Brewery was taken over by the Anheuser-Busch Brewing Association of St. Louis, the complex was used as a beer distribution depot.

Prohibition was ratified in Nebraska in 1916 and the brewery closed.

In 1989, the architectural firm of Alley Poyner restored and renovated the building for use as their office space. With its distinctive ornamentation and artistic façade, this landmark continues to provide great visual interest to the architectural landscape.

1213 Jones St.
BUILT: 1887
ARCHITECT: *Henry Voss*
STYLE: *Romanesque Revival*

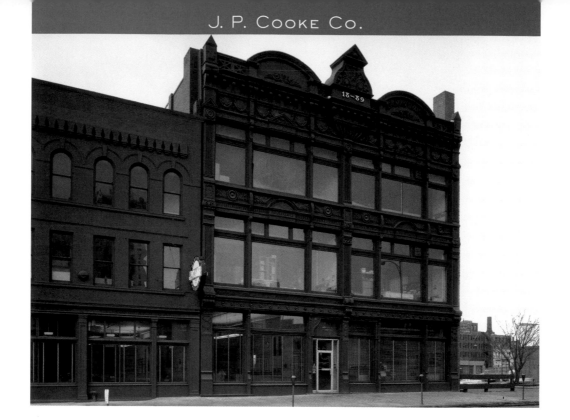

THIS THREE-STORY BRICK STRUCTURE built by Ehoman Thayer in 1889 is noted for its distinctive cast iron façade. Use of the decorative iron frame allowed for the placement of unusually large windows, uncommon at the time, giving the exterior a lighter, more open appearance. The cornice and roofline also have design elements made of metal that give the structure a distinct visual impact.

In years past, the building contained Omaha's first municipal swimming pool called the Omaha Atrium. It was accessed through an exterior stairway that led to the basement where the pool was located.

Now owned and occupied by the J. P. Cooke Co., the historic character of the original exterior is pleasing and well preserved.

1309-1315 Howard St.
BUILT: 1889
ARCHITECT: *Unknown*
STYLE: *Commercial Revival*

Listed on the National Register of Historic Places

OF GREAT SIGNIFICANCE to the architectural heritage of Omaha, the most prominent architects of the day, the New York firm of McKim, Mead and White designed this classically styled building. Completed in 1889, at a cost of $750,000, its 10 stories distinguished it as the tallest structure in Omaha. It was among the last buildings of its size to be built with massive masonry load-bearing walls.

Modeled after a Florentine palazzo with rusticated granite at the ground exterior, it has an identical twin structure in Kansas City, Missouri. The three lower floors are Massachusetts brownstone and the upper stories are hydraulic pressed brick. The façade also features decorative terra cotta trim. A large bronze eagle designed by the noted sculptor Louis Saint-Gaudens is positioned on a pediment above the high arched main entrance.

The building was purchased by the Omaha National Bank in 1909, and in 1920 an 11th story was added to the two main building masses. After World War II, an outer court was built over the second and third levels to create additional office space.

Acquired in 1977 by the law firm of Kutak, Rock and Campbell, for use as their offices, the interior has been almost entirely redesigned. The exterior façade remains unaltered.

This stately landmark is still a dominant presence in downtown Omaha and has been known in recent years as the Omaha Building.

17th and Farnam Streets
BUILT: 1889
ARCHITECT: *McKim, Mead and White*
STYLE: *Renaissance Revival*

THIS STRUCTURE was built for A. K. Riley, a local attorney and real estate developer. In 1889 it was constructed of Kesota limestone and St. Louis pressed brick for $40,000. It included the first hydraulic powered freight elevator in Omaha.

The exterior utilizes rusticated stone, as well as decorative brickwork and arched windows. These features combine both Richardson Romanesque and Queen Anne styles. The simple vertical composition and large windows are well suited for large interior spaces and give definition to the building's design.

There is a central pier running through the structure, dividing it into two equal parts. In addition, the window openings are accented by the use of steel lintels decorated with cast iron flower ornaments.

The A. K. Riley building is one of the oldest existing commercial structures in the city. It has recently been renovated and redeveloped for use by commercial tenants and is in very good condition.

1014-1016 Douglas St.
BUILT: 1889
ARCHITECT: *Smith and Ledebrink*
STYLE: *Classic Revival/Commercial*

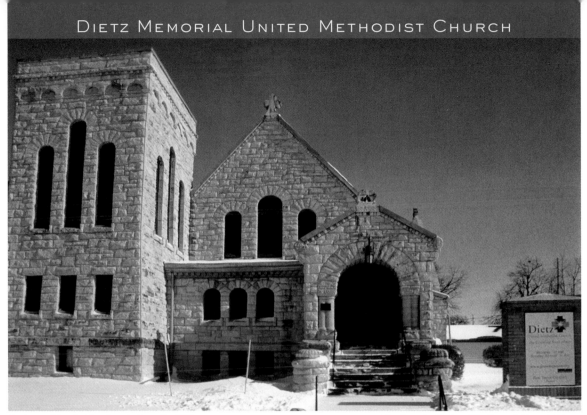

DIETZ MEMORIAL UNITED METHODIST CHURCH

Designated Omaha Landmark: Sept. 28, 1982　　　　*Listed on the National Register of Historic Places*

THIS OUTSTANDING EXAMPLE of Romanesque and Gothic style architecture has seen much history since it was built in the late 1880s. New York native and Cornell University graduate, John W. H. Hawkins designed the church after establishing an Omaha office in 1885.

The church is built entirely of Oketo Limestone. The sanctuary is laid in a cruciform design, with strong rounded arches supported by colonnades, and tall arched windows. Construction cost was $30,000. Beautiful stained glass windows are imported from London and were made by Cox, Buckley and Co. A rare tracker pipe organ built by the Wirsching Organ Co. of Salem, Ohio, dates from the original construction of the church.

Originally built as St. Mathias Episcopal Church, it was constructed as a parish church and chapel for the adjacent Brownell Hall, a female seminary operated by the Episcopal diocese.

In June 1920, when Brownell relocated, the church was sold to the Methodist congregation. The family of Gould P. Dietz, a prominent Omaha lumber dealer, helped fund the purchase.

This beautiful structure retains almost all of its original design elements, and the elegant façade provides great visual appeal.

1423 S. 10th St.
BUILT: 1889
ARCHITECT: *John W. H. Hawkins*
STYLE: *Romanesque and Gothic Revival*

Designated Omaha Landmark: Oct. 14, 1980   *Listed on the National Register of Historic Places*

ONE OF THE FEW remaining examples of authentic Queen Anne style in Omaha, this home was the first residence built in Bemis Park. Queen Anne style elements include variations of wall surfaces, a high multi-gabled roof, a rounded turret, and curved and arched windows. Prominent chimneys and Eastlake porches are other attributions.

The interior exhibits many decorative features, including oak woodwork, fireplace tiles and stained glass windows. A hand pump by the kitchen sink and working service bells in each room are original. Other period features are the sliding doors between the vestibule and the parlors and the claw foot bathtub in one of two bathrooms.

Edgar Zabriski, a native of New York, worked as a ship's officer, Civil War soldier and Union Pacific General Agent. After serving the railroad for 10 years in various locations, Zabriski established his home in Omaha about 1885. His son, Edgar Zabriski Jr., took residence in the house after the death of his father in 1908, and remained until his own passing in 1968.

The residence remains in almost original condition, to include gas light fixtures that are operational today. The only alteration to the original exterior is the removal of a bell-shaped roof that once covered the tower.

3524 Hawthorne Ave.
BUILT: 1889
ARCHITECT: *Fowler and Beindorff*
STYLE: *Queen Anne*

Designated Omaha Landmark: Jan. 28, 1986   *Listed on the National Register of Historic Places*

THE OMAHA FIRM of Mendelssohn, Fisher and Lawrie designed this 16-room Richardson Romanesque style building. The same architects designed many of the city's most important structures. Contractors were Rockford, Gould and Gladden, and construction cost was $40,000.

The school was named in honor of Charles Mason, an eminent lawyer and jurist, who served as a Justice of the Nebraska State Supreme Court and General Commissioner of Lands for Nebraska. Mason was a proponent for the establishment of the University of Nebraska, and Mason Street is named for him.

At the time the school was built, it was situated at the western edge of Omaha, on the then unpaved 24th Street. The original enrollment was 326 students, but the student population increased so rapidly that three wooden annexes were placed beside the school. These were replaced in 1936 with a brick addition attached to the original building.

The original elevations of the school remain largely unchanged despite conversion to 32 apartments in the 1980s.

1012 S. 24th St.
BUILT: 1889
ARCHITECT: *Mendelssohn, Fisher & Lawrie*
STYLE: *Richardson Romanesque*

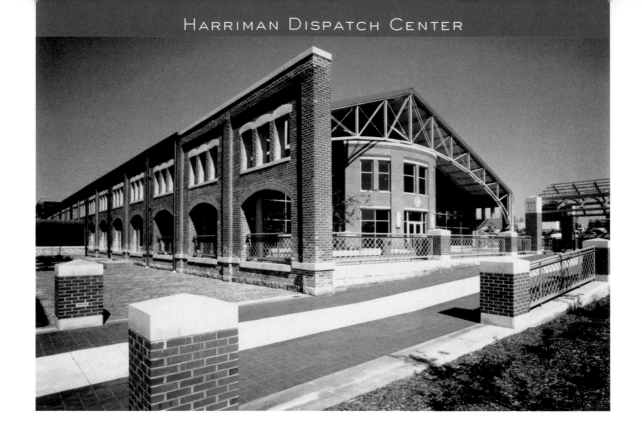

THE FIRST UNION DEPOT, designed by Alfred R. Dufrene, stood at 10th and Mason Streets, and was built in 1872. Known as "the cowshed," it was open at both ends and provided little protection. In 1890, this station was razed. Its large roof trusses were utilized in the construction of the new freight house and depot at Ninth and Jackson Streets.

Constructed of brick, with limestone trim at the windows, this was the second largest railroad depot in the country at the time of its construction in 1890. Simple and functional in design, the building was 375 feet long and was utilized for both freight and passenger service until 1900, when yet another passenger station was built at 10th and Marcy Streets.

Later used as a warehouse, the railroad discontinued using the local freight station in 1977. In 1988, as a part of the Omaha Riverfront development project, the Union Pacific Railroad redeveloped the structure into the modern Harriman Dispatch Center. The exterior was restored, although 100 feet at the east end was removed to accommodate the construction of the ConAgra campus. As a result of these modifications, the basic structure was saved and is well utilized today.

615 S. 9th St.
BUILT: 1890
ARCHITECT: *Alfred R. Dufrene*
STYLE: *Classical/Commercial*

JOSEPH GARNEAU JR./THOMAS KILPATRICK RESIDENCE

Designated Omaha Landmark: Jan. 22, 1980   *Listed on the National Register of Historic Places*

THIS STRUCTURE is an unusual surviving example of the Richardson Romanesque Revival style in Omaha. Constructed of brick and sandstone, it served first as the residence of Joseph Garneau Jr., owner of the Garneau Cracker Co.

Garneau moved to Chicago at the turn of the century, and in 1903 the house was sold to Thomas Kilpatrick, owner of a large clothing manufacturing and dry goods retailing business. His company, Thomas Kilpatrick Co., was later acquired by Younker Brothers Stores. Kilpatrick continued to reside in the home until his death in 1916.

When the house was originally built, the area in which it was located was quite remote. Only one other substantial home was nearby. Since the Kilpatrick ownership, there have been many occupants of the residence. The interior has been extensively remodeled and few original features remain.

Although the original red brick and sandstone façade has been overlaid with stucco, the robust Romanesque roofline, arches, and windows remain.

3100 Chicago St.
BUILT: 1890
ARCHITECT: *Unknown*
STYLE: *Romanesque Revival*

TASSO

SHAKSPERE

ONE OF THE MOST SIGNIFICANT structures in Nebraska, this second Renaissance Revival building is the work of noted architect Thomas R. Kimball. In its design, Kimball may have been influenced by the form of the Boston Public Library, as he was living in Boston at the time that structure was being built.

In 1891, Omaha civic leader and philanthropist Byron Reed bequeathed land to the city of Omaha on the condition that a library be constructed on the site within one year. Kimball was selected to provide the design. It was his first major commission in Omaha, and the library was completed in 1894. Because Reed's will specified that the building be fireproof, the library was built on a steel frame under solid masonry and clad in buff-colored pressed brick with extensive use of terra cotta detailing.

The structure resembles an Italian palazzo with three stories facing Harney Street and four stories in the rear, due to sloping of the lot. The raised basement facing is rusticated sandstone. Terra cotta pilasters flank the main arched doorway. The piano nobile or principal story has arched fenestration, and the attic story is surrounded by a classical cornice.

The building served as Omaha's Main Public Library until 1977. Redevelopment began in 1980 when a Wichita developer began renovation for use as office space. Reopening in August 1982, it is known today as Historic Library Plaza and remains one of Omaha's most prominent and important architectural landmarks.

1823 Harney St.
BUILT: 1892
ARCHITECT: *Thomas R. Kimball*
STYLE: *Second Renaissance Revival*

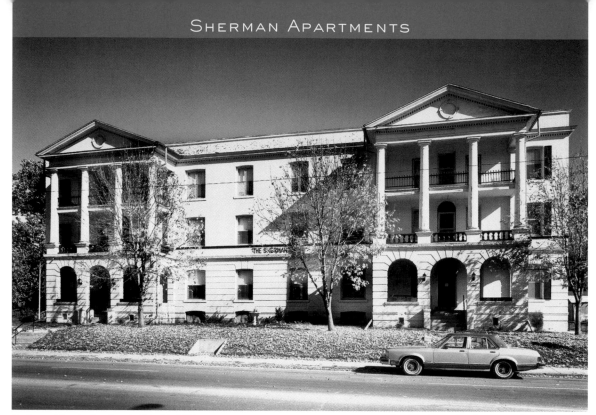

Designated Omaha Landmark: Feb. 26, 1985   *Listed on the National Register of Historic Places*

CONTRACTOR GUS PETERSON constructed this elegant and imposing three-story apartment building in 1897 for real estate developers Payne and Harder. George H. Payne was president of the Eastern Realty Co., and was responsible for a number of building projects in Omaha.

The building was named for Sherman Avenue, now 16th Street, where it is located. This location was selected due to its proximity to the north streetcar line. The building, originally the home to merchants and professional people, has been in continuous use as an apartment building since the time of its construction.

The oldest remaining apartment building in the city, it exhibits many distinct Neoclassical forms, including twin porticoes, each supported by four columns. Its design was probably influenced by the World's Colombian Exposition held in Chicago in 1893. Presently, it contains 15 apartment units.

2501 N. 16th St.
BUILT: 1897
ARCHITECT: *Frederick A. Henninger*
STYLE: *Neoclassical Revival*

Listed on the National Register of Historic Places

THE BURLINGTON RAILROAD completed construction of this terminal in 1898 and opened it on July 4th welcoming visitors to Omaha for the Trans-Mississippi and International Exposition. At the time it was considered one of the  two most outstanding examples of Greek Revival architecture in America. The other is Founders Hall at Girard College in Philadelphia.

The structure, as originally built, was thought to be one of architect Thomas R. Kimball's masterpieces. Kimball used a classic Helenic temple form, which incorporated 28 pink Colorado granite columns in the Doric style, to support the front portico.

The original interior included an 80-foot square second floor passenger waiting room appointed with Sienna marble columns and a mosaic tile floor. An artistic double spiral stairway in the center of the room provided access to the lobby on the first level.

In 1930, Graham, Anderson, Probst and White of Chicago remodeled the structure. The station was reworked in a Neoclassical Revival style and most of the original and distinctive exterior features were removed. The general appearance and roofline were considerably altered and interior renovations included the removal of the grand double staircase. The granite exterior columns were also removed and 24 of them were transported to the University of Nebraska in Lincoln, where they are arranged in an open colonnade near the stadium.

After several changes of ownership, the structure remains vulnerable and its future is uncertain.

925 S. 10th St.
BUILT: 1898
ARCHITECT: *Thomas R. Kimball*
STYLE: *Greek Revival*

Designated Omaha Landmark: Sept. 24, 1985　　　　*Listed on the National Register of Historic Places*

During his long career as an architect in Omaha, John Latenser Sr. designed dozens of school buildings. The Saunders School is a fine, early example of his signature style for public architectural design.

The school was named for Alvin M. Saunders, who served as the last Territorial Governor of Nebraska, just prior to statehood in 1867. He later resided in Omaha and served as a United States Senator from 1877 until 1883.

Closed in the spring of 1984, this brick structure faced an uncertain future. It was damaged by vandals and began to deteriorate. In the fall of 1984, a group of investors purchased it for redevelopment. Renovation had begun when the building suffered significant damage from an arsonist's fire. Notwithstanding the misfortune, the project continued and in the late 1980s work was completed for redesign of the structure for use as 21 apartments. A floor plan similar to that of the school was used and the exterior retained most of the original features. The annex was converted into two additional units.

415 N. 41st Ave.
BUILT: 1899
ARCHITECT: *John Latenser Sr.*
STYLE: *Neoclassical Revival*

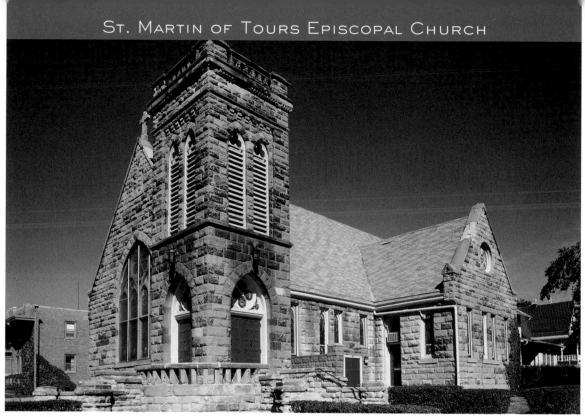

ST. MARTIN OF TOURS EPISCOPAL CHURCH

Designated Omaha Landmark: March 16, 1982

Listed on the National Register of Historic Places

ST. MARTIN OF TOURS EPISCOPAL CHURCH is the result of the confluence of two events. In the late 1880s, Dr. George L. Miller, a prominent pioneer of Omaha, constructed an immense limestone mansion known as Seymour Park, at what is now 75th and Oakwood Streets in Ralston. Misfortune struck in 1898 when his home was destroyed by a fire caused by placing kerosene lamps too close to pipes wrapped with felt to prevent freezing.

At the same time, the small congregation of St. Martin of Tours, founded as an outreach program by the Dean of Trinity Cathedral, was developing a plan to build a church. The church was built between 1899 to 1900, when the congregation was able to obtain the blocks of limestone from the ruined Miller mansion.

The building's design is consistent with a trend within the Episcopal Church at the time to stress the purity of worship by returning to the historic church architecture of the Middle Ages. St. Martin Church is a fine example of the Late Gothic Revival style of architecture.

2312 J St.
BUILT: 1899
ARCHITECT: *Unknown*
STYLE: *Late Gothic Revival*

St. Philomena's Catholic Church

1900 – 1909

Let it be such work as our descendants will thank us for...

Listed on the National Register of Historic Places

OMAHA CENTRAL HIGH SCHOOL is the oldest high school building in Omaha still in use. Historically significant, the location of the high school was the site of the Nebraska Territorial Capitol Building.

When the capitol was moved to Lincoln in 1867, the building became a school. Found to be structurally unsound, it was replaced by a large brick high school building, constructed between 1869-1872.

By 1899, Omaha High School had outgrown this structure and architect John Latenser Sr. was commissioned to design a new building. Construction of the classical limestone structure began in 1900. Built in four stages over the next 12 years, the final cost was $750,000.

The new building was constructed around the old high school, which was eventually demolished as the final wing of the new building was completed. This space formed the courtyard that became an integral part of the new high school design.

The masonry building is three levels above a full basement, supported by a steel frame with iron plate filler. The lower surface and first floor is rusticated, the upper stories are smooth ashlar block.

A two-story addition, which included the auditorium, a gym and band room, was constructed to the north of the main structure in 1930. Another addition was attached to the structure in 1978. This addition provided a second gym and more athletic facilities.

A multi-million dollar renovation and building project, scheduled for completion in 2004, will update classrooms and offices, provide a 5,200-seat stadium, and for the first time the building will have central air conditioning.

This outstanding architectural landmark continues to serve the educational needs of the community, and is very well maintained. The original façade remains intact.

124 N. 20th St.
BUILT: 1900
ARCHITECT: *John Latenser Sr.*
STYLE: *Second Renaissance Revival*

T. C. HAVENS RESIDENCE

Designated Omaha Landmark: Nov. 23, 1981 · *Listed on the National Register of Historic Places*

THOMAS COLLINS HAVENS came to Omaha in 1872, to work for the new Union Pacific Railroad. Seeking his own opportunity in this developing community, he then entered the coal business. In 1884, he founded T. C. Havens and Co. and soon added branches in Lincoln and Atchison, Kansas.

As a declaration of prosperity, Havens erected this fine home in 1900. The exterior is entirely covered in limestone, which makes this residence quite distinctive. A wide veranda supported by decorative columns surrounds the two and one-half story structure. Much oak woodwork was originally used on the interior.

T. C. Havens lived in this home until his death in 1908. The house was later sold to Walter T. Page, the manager of the American Smelting and Refining Co. Through the years there have been several additional owners, and the interior has experienced modifications. The classical and elegant façade, however, remains basically unchanged.

101 N. 39th St.
BUILT: 1900
ARCHITECT: *Frederick A. Henninger*
STYLE: *Second Renaissance Revival*

THIS IMPOSING RESIDENCE, built for Freeman P. Kirkendall, owner of the Kirkendall Boot Co., is an outstanding example of residential design by Thomas R. Kimball and ranks among the largest of the Gold Coast homes.

An impressive statement is made by the elongated main façade. The house is constructed of load bearing buff brick with extensive use of decorative stone trim. Rectangular in shape, a unique upper story exhibits panels of variegated green marble. There is a brick corbel table and a prominent roofline. Recessed brick at the first level creates a rusticated effect and limestone is used to accent window openings. The overall design is intended to resemble an Italian palazzo, giving the appearance of restrained strength. The same decorative elements are incorporated in the detached carriage house/garage.

In later years the home was divided into apartments, however, the present owners have undertaken careful renovation, returning it to a single-family dwelling.

The Omaha Symphony selected the house as the 2003 Omaha Symphony/ASID Designer Showhouse.

3727 Jackson St.
BUILT: 1901
ARCHITECT: *Thomas R. Kimball*
STYLE: *Second Renaissance Revival*

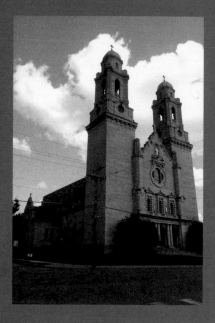

This MAGNIFICENT structure is one of Omaha's most beautiful and significant architectural achievements. It is the masterwork of architect Thomas R. Kimball. One of the 10 largest Catholic cathedrals in America, it stands atop a hill north of Omaha's historic Gold Coast area.

Kimball began work on the design in 1901, incorporating many features associated with the Spanish colonial period. This outstanding example of Spanish Revival style is a very early adaptation of the style in America.

Construction commenced in 1905 and by 1907 work had progressed to the point that an elaborate ceremony was held to lay the cornerstone. First services in the uncompleted sanctuary were held in December 1916. Bishop Richard Scannel dictated that construction proceed only as funds were available. For this reason, it required more than 50 years to complete the cathedral.

The church was constructed using a steel frame under solid masonry walls that are faced with Bedford limestone. The roof is red Spanish tile. Identical domed cupolas terminate the twin towers which rise to a height of 187 feet. These were not completed until 1959, just prior to the consecration of the Cathedral. The high vertical surface of the main façade imparts a perception of strength and stability.

Massive buttresses employing volutes surround the exterior of the nave. The triple portal with great bronze doors, separated by Tuscan columns, provides entrance to the vestibule.

The interior consists of a nave without transept. The sanctuary is covered by a huge barrel vaulted ceiling with supporting ribs, designed as a series of double-arched bays. The church can accommodate 1,000 seated parishioners.

Installed in 1919, the sanctuary is dominated by a high altar of white Carrara marble with elaborate carved wooden cathedra, screen and clerical stalls.

Kimball himself designed the pulpit and confessionals, which were then custom made in Pietrasanta, Italy. Boston artist, Charles J. Connick, created the windows, and Albin Polasek, of Czechoslovakia, did much of the beautiful woodcarving. Exceptional works of art and architectural design are to be found throughout this marvelous structure. Extensive interior renovation was completed in 2002.

701 N. 40th St.
BUILT: 1905
ARCHITECT: *Thomas R. Kimball*
STYLE: *Spanish Renaissance Revival*

THE FIRST ST. MARY MAGDELENE CHURCH was built in 1868 at 17th and Douglas Streets. In 1873 a second frame building was constructed to house the church's school. Both were destroyed by fire on Feb. 3, 1894, and rebuilt shortly thereafter.

In 1902, construction of this new church began at 19th and Dodge Streets and the structure was dedicated in 1903.

The location of the present church is historically significant as it was originally the site of the home of the territorial governor of Nebraska, Thomas B. Cuming. The very first Mass in the new city of Omaha was celebrated May 15, 1855, in the parlor of his house.

In 1919, an extensive grading project to lower the elevation of Dodge Street necessitated the church's reconstruction. Omaha architect, John Latenser Sr. supervised the rebuilding of the church and an entirely new substructure was built beneath the existing church. The work was completed in time for Christmas, 1920.

This Gothic style church is buff brick with stone trim. Crosses stand above the peaked gables. Stepped buttress-type columns mark the wall corners and the tower corners of the church. The building contains two sets of magnificent stained glass windows from Munich, Germany installed in 1902, and in 1920. It is in excellent condition and is a treasure to the downtown streetscape.

109 S. 19th St.
BUILT: 1903
ARCHITECT: *Unknown*
STYLE: *Gothic Revival*

Designated Omaha Landmark: March 17, 1992   *Listed on the National Register of Historic Places*

THE EGGERSS-O'FLYNG CO. was a major manufacturer of cardboard boxes and containers in Omaha for more than 50 years.

The original three-story building was designed by Joseph P. Guth and built in 1902. Over the next 26 years, there were three major additions. The original section, constructed of brick with load-bearing walls, was used as a warehouse.

Guth was commissioned to design two additional extensions as the company grew. The first section, built in 1912, was six new levels to the east of the original building. In 1918, a three-story addition was erected.

By 1928 even more space was needed and John Latenser Sr. designed a new four-story addition south of the original structure.

As is the case with a number of former downtown Omaha commercial structures, the Eggerss-O'Flyng Building has undergone redesign and re-development for use as residential space.

801 S. 15th St.
BUILT: 1902
ARCHITECT: *J. P. Guth*
STYLE: *Renaissance Revival*

Designated Omaha Landmark: March 17, 1981   *Listed on the National Register of Historic Places*

CONTRACTOR WILLIAM RICE built this large elegant residence in the Bemis Park neighborhood at a cost of $3,000 for Dr. Elmer Porter, a prominent Omaha physician.

Constructed of wood, this house is one and one-half stories on a brick foundation. Broad eves with central hipped roof dormers on the north and south sides are prominent features. Five bay porches terminate in a porte-cochere on the southwest corner and are designed to let vehicles pass from the street to the interior courtyard.

Distinctive interior features include a set of landscape murals painted by Gustave A. Fuchs, an artist from Germany. Fuchs and his brothers originally came to Omaha to do several church commissions.

The home was occupied from 1923 to 1970, by Arthur C. Thomsen, dean of the University of Omaha Law School, editor of the "Night Law Bulletin," and a District Court judge from 1928 until 1961.

The house remains a private, single family residence and is in good condition today.

3426 Lincoln Blvd.
BUILT: 1902
ARCHITECT: *Frederick A. Henninger*
STYLE: *Georgian Revival*

Designated Omaha Landmark: April 17, 1979   *Listed on the National Register of Historic Places*

BUILT ON LAND DONATED by Kountze Place developer, Herman Kountze, this outstanding example of the Late Gothic Revival style was the design of prominent Omaha architects George Fisher and Harry Lawrie.

The church was designed in 1900, and construction completed in 1902. With its tall spire, it soon became a prominent landmark in the area. The cost of the finished church was $25,000, most of it obtained through various fund raising activities of the congregation. Dedication of the new church was held June 8, 1902, and was attended by many prominent Omahans.

From the exterior, important Gothic Revival elements can be seen. Rock-faced coursed ashlar walls of Colorado lava stone and Bedford limestone are punctuated by elongated lancet windows.

The basic floor plan is the form of a Latin cross, and a steeply pitched, gabled roof of slate covers the whole. The most striking exterior feature of the building is the tower and spire that achieves a height of 124 feet. A one story side chapel extends from the southwest corner.

Within the interior, elaborate stenciling on the vaults of the transepts and hand painted scenes can be seen. Gothic white oak paneled confessionals and screens flank the sanctuary.

An important landmark in this historic Omaha neighborhood, Sacred Heart Church is well maintained and in good condition today.

2206 Binney St.
BUILT: 1902
ARCHITECTS: *Fisher and Lawrie*
STYLE: *Late Gothic Revival*

GEORGE A. JOSLYN RESIDENCE/JOSLYN CASTLE

Designated Omaha Landmark: May 22, 1979

Listed on the National Register of Historic Places

NAMED LYNHURST AT THE TIME of its construction in 1903, the house is better known as the Joslyn Castle. This truly magnificent and unique structure is today considered one of the city's most prominent and well-known architectural landmarks.

Omaha architect John McDonald designed it for George A. and Sarah H. Joslyn. Although the design incorporates numerous styles, it has most often been described as Scottish Baronial.

Built entirely of Vermont Silverdale limestone, the house contains 35 rooms. The stone was delivered in large slabs and each block was cut on site. Two stone turrets accent opposite corners of the three-story structure. A wrought iron front door weighs nearly a ton and hangs in a marble frame.

Construction began in 1902 and took 11 months to complete. The Joslyn's then hired the firm of Sperling and Linden of Chicago to decorate the interior at a cost of more than $50,000. Appointments are as lavish and decorative as those of the exterior.

The vestibule has a mosaic tile floor. Walls, ceiling, and the main entry hall and rounded staircase are Spanish mahogany. Mahogany, walnut, oak, and bird's-eye maple woodwork are used throughout. Stained glass windows, painted ceilings, leaded glass cabinets, and a gold-leafed frieze are some of the appointments that reflect the desire of the Joslyns' to include the best of the decorative arts in their home.

The only major addition to the house after construction is a music room added to the west side in 1906. It was built with a high ceiling to accommodate pipes for the player organ.

George A. Joslyn died in 1916. Upon the passing of Mrs. Joslyn in 1940, the home became the property of the Society of Liberal Arts. It was later leased and then sold to the Omaha Board of Education and used for offices. Upon being vacated by the Board of Education, the property was acquired by the State of Nebraska who administers and maintains it today.

3902 Davenport St.
BUILT: 1903
ARCHITECT: *John McDonald*
STYLE: *Scottish Baronial*

Designated Omaha Landmark: July 14, 1981

ARCHITECT AND BUILDER GEORGE F. SHEPARD designed this stately transitional style home as his personal residence.

Shepard built the home for $10,000 using brick with wood and stone trim. An accomplished stone mason and artist, Shepard devoted much attention to the design and detailing of his residence. He had been a marble cutter by trade, and personally executed many of the stone ornaments, including a front step incised with his name.

His residence was one of the finer structures built in the newly developed Kountze Place Addition. The house has been well maintained.

1802 Wirt St.
BUILT: 1903
ARCHITECT: *George F. Shepard*
STYLE: *Queen Anne/Beaux Arts*

DUNDEE ELEMENTARY SCHOOL

THE DUNDEE SCHOOL began in a small wood structure at 4908 California St. in the 1890s. That building was sold, and a new school was built in 1904 to accommodate the rapid development of the Village of Dundee.

The new structure was constructed of tan brick and contained six classrooms. By 1909, enrollment had grown to 150, and an addition was built which contained eight more rooms. Continued growth required a second addition in 1915, providing additional classroom space as well as a gymnasium and auditorium.

Dundee School was incorporated into the Omaha Public Schools upon annexation of the village June 20, 1915.

One of the distinctive architectural features is a bell tower on the roof, which was part of the original design. In 1946, the bell was silenced, as it was feared the vibrations would damage the roof. Through the years, there have been numerous interior renovations. In 1975, the bell tower was repaired, thus allowing the bell to be used again on special occasions.

In 1993, a $6 million renovation began and was completed in 1995. Many modern features were included. The original oak floors were also refinished at that time.

310 N. 51st St.
BUILT: 1904
ARCHITECT: *D. Finlayson*
STYLE: *Neoclassical Revival*

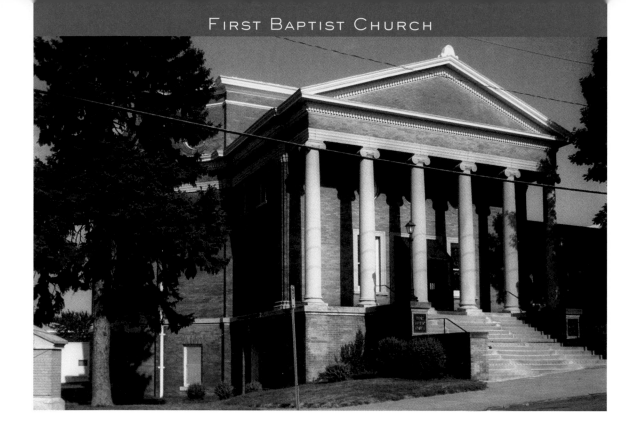

CONSTRUCTION ON THIS BEAUTIFUL classically designed structure began in 1903, and was completed October 1904 for $44,500. The overall design of the church is cruciform. The buff brick construction is highlighted by much use of Bedford limestone.

The most outstanding exterior feature of the church is a 33-foot portico with an imposing triangular pediment supported by six limestone Ionic columns. An octagonal dome surmounts the main sanctuary.

In 1924, the McDonald firm was commissioned to design an addition to the south. Complimenting the original classical design, it contains classrooms, offices, community use areas and a gymnasium.

The gymnasium was remodeled in 1940, and in 1948 an air conditioning system was installed thus making First Baptist the first church structure in Omaha to enjoy this luxury.

The interior has been remodeled and redecorated several times through the years, however, the original integrity of the classical design has been carefully maintained.

421 Park Ave.
BUILT: 1904
ARCHITECTS: *Main Bldg - John McDonald;*
1924 Addition - John and Alan McDonald
STYLE: *Classical Revival*

THE CONGREGATION of the Kountze Memorial Lutheran Church can trace their history in Omaha to Dec. 5, 1858, at which time the congregation officially organized as the first Lutheran church in Omaha. First meeting at 13th and Douglas Streets, they then constructed a new church at 16th and Harney Streets in 1883. Commercial development began to crowd the building, and it was sold in 1904. The congregation then purchased the site at 26th and Farnam Streets and arranged to build again.

John H. Harte, an Omaha contractor, assisted with building plans and later supervised construction of the new structure. The architectural firm of Turnbull and Jones of Elgin, Illinois were selected to provide the design. The cornerstone was laid Sept. 25, 1905, and the completed building was dedicated on Sunday, May 27, 1906.

Built almost entirely of Bedford limestone, the structure is distinguished by a tall bell tower. The interior features a circular sanctuary and curved pews with a magnificent skylight and unique side apse. All of the woodwork is solid quartersawn oak and many beautiful stained glass windows are present.

The church is named in honor of the family of Herman Kountze, who provided the largest contribution for the first building and a significant gift for the new church.

The elegant German Gothic design of this church is an important contribution to the architectural landscape of Omaha today.

2650 Farnam St.
BUILT: 1904
ARCHITECT: *Turnbull and Jones*
STYLE: *Gothic Revival*

BRANDEIS/MILLARD RESIDENCE

Designated Omaha Landmark: June 10, 1986   *Listed on the National Register of Historic Places*

NATIONALLY RECOGNIZED ARCHITECT Albert Kahn (1869-1942) of Detroit, Michigan designed this spacious and attractive home for Arthur and Zerlina Brandeis, members of the family that owned the Brandeis department store. It is the only existing structure in Nebraska designed by Kahn.

Kahn is especially well known for his industrial designs. In Detroit, he was responsible for the complex of structures that make up the Ford Motor Co. factory at Willow Run. He also designed the entire manufacturing complex for Packard Motor Co., as well as an elegant mansion for Edsel Ford.

A very fine example of the Jacobethan style, no expense was spared on either exterior finishing or interior detailing. The primary construction material is brick with extensive limestone trim. The house and carriage house are both covered with a red tile roof.

In 1909, the home was sold to Jessie H. Millard as a residence for herself and her father, Senator Joseph H. Millard. He was a prominent political and business leader in Omaha. At the time he moved into this home, he was also president of the Omaha National Bank.

The Millard family resided here until 1922, and from that point there have been several owners. Once again utilized as a single family dwelling, this elaborate Gold Coast mansion is being sensitively restored and renovated by the present owners.

500 S. 38th St.
BUILT: 1904
ARCHITECT: *Albert Kahn*
STYLE: *Jacobethan Revival*

Listed on the National Register of Historic Places

THE STREHLOW TERRACE apartment complex is an early example of 20th century apartment building design and site planning. It is Nebraska's first known example of an integrated grouping of related apartment buildings.

Six buildings make up the group; three multi-unit apartment houses, the Majestic, the Strehlow, and the Roland built in 1905, 1907 and 1909, respectively. A one-story annex/apartment, a two-story residence and a garage/apartment were built between 1910 and 1916.

Contractor Robert C. Strehlow used his experience as superintendent of construction for the Trans-Mississippi and International Exposition of 1898 to create this unique complex of apartments. Built of buff brick, the structures are arranged around a central courtyard with a concrete fountain and benches, which remain today.

The central court arrangement, decorative sculptured fountain, and landscaped grounds were probably inspired by turn-of-the century Exposition designs.

The buildings stand vacant today and their future is uncertain.

2024 and 2107 N. 16th St.
BUILT: 1905
ARCHITECT: *Frederick A. Henninger*
STYLE: *Eclectic*

CHARLES D. McLAUGHLIN RESIDENDE

Designated Omaha Landmark: March 16, 1982

Listed on the National Register of Historic Places

THIS SPACIOUS BRICK HOME was originally built for manufacturer Charles D. McLaughlin. It is a fine example of the transition to a simple, more refined architectural form following the Victorian period. Due to demand for a more ordered system of design and ornamentation, many architects began to pursue a classical American style, inspired by early American architecture.

The McDonald architectural firm was a leader in this style in Omaha, and this Colonial Revival style house incorporates much of the period trend. The McDonald firm designed both the Joslyn Art Museum and the Joslyn Castle.

Situated in the affluent Gold Coast area, the residence has had several owners in addition to McLaughlin. E. E. Bruce, a prominent local businessman and Dr. R. Russell Best, a nationally known professor of anatomy and surgery, were subsequent residents. The house is in very good condition.

507 S. 38th St.
BUILT: 1905
ARCHITECT: *John McDonald*
STYLE: *Colonial Revival*

Designated Omaha Landmark: April 17, 1979

THIS INTERESTING HOME was constructed in 1905 by Gustave F. Epeneter, owner of the Eagle Cornice Works. The initial cost was $2,500. It is done in a basic style that was popular at the time, and was something of a departure from the earlier Queen Anne and Victorian trends that used extravagant detail and ornamentation.

The most distinctive feature of the exterior is a galvanized iron balustrade railing placed atop the hip roof, imparting a dramatic design style to the roofline. A stamped metal frieze runs along the cornice line.

The front entrance is set beneath a portico extending across the house, and is emphasized by a central projecting pediment located directly below a second story bay window.

Epeneter utilized materials which were made in his factory whenever possible, which adds interest to the interior finishing. A ballroom dominates the third level. Oak woodwork is used throughout the interior. The Epeneter family sold the home in 1912, and there have been several subsequent owners. However, much of the original character and design can still be found on both the exterior and interior of this classic-box structure.

502 N. 40th St.
BUILT: 1905
BUILDER: *G. F. Epeneter*
STYLE: *Classic Box*

GOTTLIEB STORZ RESIDENCE

Designated Omaha Landmark: Dec. 21, 1982

Listed on the National Register of Historic Places

GOTTLIEB STORZ emigrated from his native Germany in 1872 to ply his trade as a brewer. During the next four years, he worked in New York and St. Louis, and finally located in Omaha to establish the Storz Brewing Co.

Today, his elegant Gold Coast mansion is a reminder of his success in an adopted community. Constructed of beige brick with decorative limestone trim, the house features a red tile roof, steep gables, rectangular windows with stone mullions and transoms, all set in a symmetrical façade.

Many of the exquisite interior features remain, including hand carved oak woodwork, and a solarium covered by a magnificent stained glass dome. Both living room and dining room have distinctive mosaic fireplaces.

Until 2002, only members of the Storz family occupied this home. As a result, the original design of the house has never been altered, including the original carriage house located behind the main residence. Creighton University is the current owner.

3708 Farnam St.
BUILT: 1905
ARCHITECT: *Fisher and Lawrie*
STYLE: *Jacobethan Revival*

Designated Omaha Landmark: April 2, 1996　　　　　*Listed on the National Register of Historic Places*

OMAHA ARCHITECT Thomas R. Kimball designed this eclectic home for his mother, Mary Rogers Kimball, and his sister, Arabel M. Kimball. It occupies a historic site, once the location of St. Mary's Convent and School, from which St. Mary's Avenue takes its name. The Kimballs purchased these lots in 1903.

The house consists of two and one-half stories over a raised full basement and is constructed with load-bearing masonry walls. Built of gray Omaha pressed brick, and accented with Bedford limestone trim and details, the whole is topped with a red Spanish tile roof. Facing south, the symetrical façade is distinguished by a large stepped parapet cross gable with limestone finials. The roof is steeply pitched and accented by two additional cross gables with parapet walls on the north side.

All of the original interior features remain, and there is extensive use of oak and mahogany woodwork thoughout. The living room includes a crested hand-carved marble fireplace and leaded-glass bookcases.

In 1922, St. Mary's Avenue was graded and lowered 10 feet. Kimball then constructed a stone retaining wall with entrance gate at the street level.

The house has had only three owners. The Kimball family sold the property in 1943 and the second owners used it in multiple unit fashion. The present owner has returned it to a single-family residence. There is a carriage house of similar design and construction located at the rear of the property that is used as a garage.

Today, it is the only remaining example of the numerous fine residences that once graced St. Mary's Avenue.

2236 St. Mary's Ave.
BUILT: 1905
ARCHITECT: *Thomas R. Kimball*
STYLE: *North European Renaissance Revival*

JONAS L. BRANDEIS arrived in Omaha, and opened his first store at 506 S. 13th St., named The Fair. His mercantile business prospered, and in 1888 he opened the Boston Store on the northwest corner of 16th and Douglas Streets. In 1905, the J. L. Brandeis and Sons company began construction of a larger and more magnificent store on the southwest corner of 16th and Douglas Streets. It became a focal point of retailing in downtown Omaha for decades to come. Construction was completed in 1906. The original eight-story structure cost $650,000. In 1921, two more floors were added, costing an additional $120,000.

The building is one entire block long and one-half block wide. It was constructed on a steel frame and is faced with Bedford lime-

Listed on the National Register of Historic Places

stone, brick and terra cotta. Each exterior floor level carries separate design features. A balustrade and the projecting cornices enhance the upper stories.

Within the interior, convenience, comfort and visual appeal was emphasized. Large fluted Corinthian columns dominated the first floor area. Escalators and air conditioning were installed long before other merchants used them.

After the store closed, due to a decline in downtown retail activity, the building was sold to a developer in 1980. The first two floors were converted for commercial use, and the upper floors to office space.

The beautiful façade is still one of the dominant features of downtown Omaha.

16th and Douglas Streets
BUILT: 1906
ARCHITECT: *John Latenser Sr.*
STYLE: *Second Renaissance Revival*

PARLIN, ORENDORFF AND MARTIN PLOW CO. BUILDING

Designated Omaha Landmark: Sept. 20, 1994　　　　　*Listed on the National Register of Historic Places*

THE UNUSUAL TRAPEZOIDAL DESIGN of this large warehouse building is due to rail lines that originally ran along the south side of the building. The seven-story façade is red brick with brick and limestone detailing. The main entrance on the east side is positioned at the third level, to align with the 10th Street Bridge.

Pavilions at the east and west ends contain more detailing than the central part of the structure and are accented by arcades of recessed windows and rounded arches. Three limestone medallions decorate each side.

This structure is associated with the wholesale jobbing trade in Omaha and was built for the Parlin, Orendorff and Martin Plow Co. of Canton, Illinois, a distributor of farm implements. In 1920, the warehouse was sold to the International Harvester Co., which occupied the building until 1950. Subsequent tenants were Paxton & Gallagher Wholesale Groceries, until 1964, then the Butternut Coffee Co. until 1991.

Virtually all of the architectural design elements remain intact today, including the original cast iron and glass entry. In 2000, NuStyle Development completed a renovation of the building changing it into the Old Market Apartments, with 200 one-, two- and three-bedroom units that range from 650 to 1,300 square feet.

The building is also known as the Butternut Building.

707 S. 11th St.
BUILT: 1906
ARCHITECT: *John Latenser Sr.*
STYLE: *Renaissance Revival*

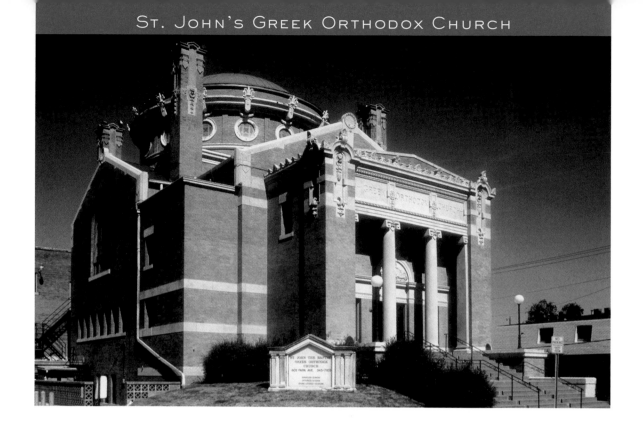

ST. JOHN'S WAS ORIGINALLY BUILT as a synagogue for the reformed Jewish congregation of Temple Israel at a cost of $50,000. Built with buff brick and extensive trim rendered in Bedford limestone, a large Byzantine style dome tops the entire structure. The auditorium and gallery were arranged to seat 600.

In 1951, Temple Israel moved to 70th and Cass Streets and St. John's Greek Orthodox Church purchased the structure rather than build on previously acquired property on St. Mary's Avenue.

The Byzantine style of this building provided an adaptable setting for the Orthodox Christian congre-

gation. The interior oak woodwork, including pews and two large stained glass windows, remains from the original decoration.

The exterior was repaired and refurbished in 1980, maintaining the unique and decorative façade. In 1981, the exterior of the dome was replaced with gold-colored sheet metal. Today, the interior features are highlighted by a large mural of Christ on the inside of the dome and an intricately carved wood icon screen between the congregation and the altar.

602 Park Ave.
BUILT: 1907
ARCHITECT: *John Latenser Sr.*
STYLE: *Exotic Revival*

REINHOLD B. BUSCH RESIDENCE

THIS SUBSTANTIAL HOME was designed by John Latenser Sr. for R. B. Busch, owner of the Omaha branch of the Crane Supply Co.

Two and one-half stories high, this home is 40′ x 57′ and was constructed of brown load-bearing brick at a cost of $20,000. A low-hipped roof, a massive medallion cornice, and carved limestone panels set into a frieze embellish the exterior. There is a large central limestone balcony with balusters. A massive double-door entry is located on the north bay porch with a cast-iron porte-cochere.

Within the structure, the use of solid oak and mahogany woodwork is extensive. The living room and spacious entry hall exhibit beautifully detailed molded ceilings.

Although the home has had several owners, it has always been well maintained and is in very good condition. From the standpoint of design and setting, it is one of the most distinctive and interesting homes in the north Gold Coast.

604 N. 38th St.
BUILT: 1907
ARCHITECT: *John Latenser Sr.*
STYLE: *Italian Renaissance Revival*

PACKERS NATIONAL BANK

PACKERS   NATIONAL   BANK

Designated Omaha Landmark: Sept. 18, 1984   *Listed on the National Register of Historic Places*

AN INFLUENTIAL INSTITUTION in South Omaha since its founding in 1891, the Packers National Bank expanded with the growing economy generated by the meat packing industry.

This attractive structure, designed in 1907 by architect Thomas R. Kimball, is a fine example of his work. Interesting features that are readily apparant on this building include a pedimented entry portico, a classical entablature, grilled balustrade, and the heavily rusticated arched windows.

In 1979 the bank vacated the building. After a time, the structure was renovated and converted into office and residential space which remains the case today. This beautiful building is in good condition and its historic façade of brick and decorative limestone trim is unaltered and greatly enhances the streetscape.

4939 S. 24th St.
BUILT: 1907
ARCHITECT: *Thomas R. Kimball*
STYLE: *Second Renaissance Revival*

Designated Omaha Landmark: Oct. 17, 1978

Listed on the National Register of Historic Places

AT THE TURN OF THE 20TH CENTURY, the M. E. Smith Co. was the largest wholesale dry goods distribution firm in Omaha.

In 1905 Catherine B. Nash commissioned architect Thomas R. Kimball to design two identical large modern warehouse buildings. Completed for $190,000, Nash immediately leased them to the M. E. Smith Co.

Each structure was eight stories high over a raised basement level. The cost of construction included full fire safety equipment and an automatic sprinkler system – the first warehouse in Omaha to be equipped in this manner.

Structurally, the Nash Block combines the necessary elements of substantial commercial architecture. However, the appearance is considerably elevated by the architect's use of arched brick-work below the roof eves, a row of arched windows on the upper level, and the heavy belt of limestone at the main floor elevation. The second, and northernmost of the two buildings was razed to facilitate construction of the Eugene Leahy Central Park Mall.

The remaining building is, from a design perspective, a simple and well-executed Renaissance Revival style composition.

In the late 1930s, a New York wholesale drug company established operations in Omaha and occupied the Nash Block. Later known as the McKesson and Robbins Drug Co., they remained here until their relocation to La Vista in 1979.

In 1989, the building was renovated for use as residential apartment units, known as The Greenhouse, and lower level commercial space. The imposing original façade has been well maintained.

902-912 Farnam St.
BUILT: 1907
ARCHITECT: *Thomas R. Kimball*
STYLE: *Renaissance Revival/Commercial*

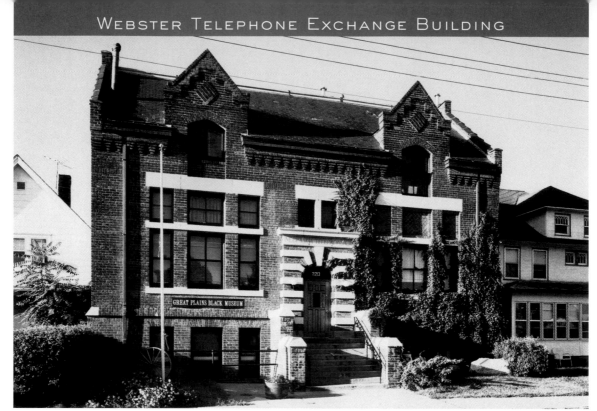

Designated Omaha Landmark: Oct. 14, 1980   *Listed on the National Register of Historic Places*

BUILT IN AN L-SHAPE the Webster Telephone Exchange Building stands one and one-half stories above a raised basement. Constructed of brick, with limestone trim, it was one of several telephone exchanges that Thomas R. Kimball designed for the Nebraska Telephone Co.

In 1933, the building was donated to the Omaha Chapter of the Urban League for use as the Mid-City Community Center. After the center closed, it was remodeled into a 16-unit apartment building in 1952. In 1970 the building again became a community center and it was donated in 1975 for use as the Great Plains Black Museum.

As a result of the numerous changes, nothing of the original interior remains. The exterior, however, still retains much of its historic and artistic integrity.

2213 Lake St.
BUILT: 1907
ARCHITECT: *Thomas R. Kimball*
STYLE: *Jacobethan Revival*

Designated Omaha Landmark: Feb. 13, 1979   *Listed on the National Register of Historic Places*

THIS OUTSTANDING RENDITION of the Spanish Renaissance Revival style is considered one of the best examples of the work of architect Thomas R. Kimball.

Constructed with a steel frame, the building is composed of piers faced with brick and stucco, projecting through the roof surface. The limestone façade is asymmetrical, with the placement of an octagonal copper-domed bell tower at the southwest corner. Extensive use of decorative Bedford limestone and a red Spanish tile roof add much to the exterior composition.

Wood rafters and beams and a ceiling of dark-stained tongue-and-groove paneling are noteworthy interior features. The Carrara marble altar was moved from the original church at 9th and Harney Streets. Magnificent stained glass windows are from Munich, Germany and were used originally in the Chapel at St. Joseph's Hospital.

This church held Cathedral status from 1908 until 1916, at which time the authority was transferred to the newly constructed St. Cecilia's on North 40th Street.

In 1958, the canonization of St. Philomena was nullified, and the church was re-named St. Francis Cabrini, in honor of Mother Cabrini, the first American citizen to be declared a Saint of the Catholic Church.

In 1910, a brick and stucco rectory, also designed by Kimball, was constructed behind the church to the east.

1335 S. 10th St.
BUILT: 1908
ARCHITECT: *Thomas R. Kimball*
STYLE: *Spanish Renaissance Revival*

Designated Omaha Landmark: June 12, 1990

Listed on the National Register of Historic Places

ALTHOUGH SEVERAL Tudor-style schools were built in Omaha, Vinton School, constructed in 1908, is the earliest and most elaborate example. Frederick W. Clarke used many Tudor and Elizabethan motifs to lend character and visual interest to his design.

Constructed primarily of brick, the two-story structure is rectangular in form with a system of load-bearing walls to realize the design concept and to support the wood joist floors. Hipped roofs within parapet walls cap the structure.

An Omaha architect, Clarke's most significant and ambitious work was the Omaha Public School District's largest facility, Omaha Technical High School.

Vinton School is one of a number of former school buildings that were sold by the school district. Although many interior alterations have been made, the developers were careful to preserve the integrity of the original façade. The building presently is used for residential apartments units.

2120 Deer Park Blvd.
BUILT: 1908
ARCHITECT: *Frederick W. Clarke*
STYLE: *Tudor Revival*

JUDGE ARTHUR ENGLISH and his wife Belle commissioned their friend John McDonald to design a home in the Cathedral neighborhood on the southeast corner of 38th and California Streets. The result is this two and one-half story structure constructed of brick. It exhibits especially strong Prairie School design features, unique to McDonald's general body of work.

Exhibiting the true concept of horizontal massing, the house is anchored by tapered brick corner piers, and rusticated granite blocks at the foundation. A suspended canopy covers a wide spacious entry flanked by two large arched windows. The roof is green clay schoolhouse tile, and copper is used for trim and downspouts. The overall appearance is one of substance and stability. The home has 14 rooms and four bathrooms.

Omaha attorney and founding partner of the firm of Kennedy, Holland, DeLacy and McLaughlin, James A. C. Kennedy and his wife Caroline purchased the house in 1923. After living there more than 50 years, the house was sold to the present owners. The building has been well cared for and is in excellent condition today.

521 N. 38th St.
BUILT: 1908
ARCHITECT: *John McDonald*
STYLE: *Modified Prairie School*

PAXTON AND GALLAGHER, once Omaha's leading grocery wholesaler, began operation in Omaha in 1870 as Creighton and Gallagher.

The principals were Ben Gallagher and John A. Creighton. Creighton left the partnership, and in 1879 William A. Paxton joined Gallagher, and the new company became Paxton and Gallagher. Business prospered, followed by expansion and construction of five large warehouses to store a variety of goods from groceries and hardware to wine and liquor. In 1908, local architect Thomas R. Kimball designed this distinctive warehouse, later known as the Butternut Building. It is constructed of red brick with a long row of arched windows along the roofline that adds much interest to the building façade.

As constructed, railroad trackage approached the building from the east, and a large opening allowed train cars to enter the dock area within the structure to load and unload. This warehouse space is a fine example of the commercial architecture that characterized many buildings in Omaha's original wholesale district.

Today, this graceful and interesting former warehouse is undergoing rehabilitation to add another dimension of use to an already revitalized downtown.

901-909 Jones St.
BUILT: 1908
ARCHITECT: *Thomas R. Kimball*
STYLE: *Classic Revival Commercial*

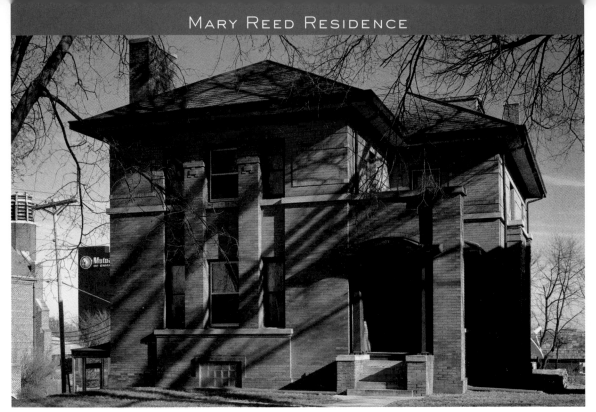

Designated Omaha Landmark: March 16, 1982

THIS OUTSTANDING EXAMPLE of Prairie School design, located in the Gold Coast district, was built for Mary Reed, the widow of Byron Reed.

Byron Reed was an Omaha pioneer real estate developer and philanthropist. At the time of his death in the early 1890s, Reed had accumulated one of the most substantial fortunes in the city in addition to one of the most important collections of coins, books and manuscripts in the United States. This collection was left to the city of Omaha.

Reed's wife, Mary, survived him by many years and was one of Omaha's oldest pioneers, living until the 1940s.

Built of brick with limestone trim, this home exhibits unusual Prairie School features, such as decorative brickwork and leaded glass windows. The exterior façade remains largely unaltered and retains much of the original design and detail.

503 S. 36th St.
BUILT: 1909
ARCHITECT: *Frederick A. Henninger*
STYLE: *Prairie School*

BRECKENRIDGE/GORDON RESIDENCE

Designated Omaha Landmark: July 6, 1982   *Included in a Historic District Listed on the National Register of Historic Places*

THIS RESIDENCE WAS BUILT for Ralph W. Breckenridge, a prominent Omaha attorney, who served as president of the Nebraska Bar Association in 1905.

Thomas R. Kimball designed the stately classic Georgian Revival house in a mature, yet restrained example of the popular style. The brick structure has a hip roof covered in slate shingles. A Palladian window appears in the dormer on third floor and there are arched windows on the second floor. The elegant front porch with a pediment, and embellished with Ionic columns, is another distinctive feature.

In August 1913, Breckenridge was the victim of an unfortunate accident, in which his own automobile killed him as he attempted to start it with the crank. That same year, his daughter Almyra wed Alfred W. Gordon, and the couple moved into the home with her mother. Mrs. Breckenridge subsequently sold the house to the Gordon's in 1930.

The property was sold by the Gordon family in 1947 and was converted to a multiple unit dwelling in 1950. The interior floor plan has undergone numerous changes over time, but the exterior retains many of the details for which Kimball is well known.

3611 Jackson St.
BUILT: 1909
ARCHITECT: *Thomas R. Kimball*
STYLE: *Georgian Revival*

Designated Omaha Landmark: April 2, 1981

THESE ELEGANT residential apartments were designed and built by a developer from Clarinda, Iowa, William W. Welch. Constructed of brick with decorative trim, they are excellent examples of the Georgian Revival style.

Welch was noted for his construction of institutional buildings in Iowa at the time of construction of these apartments in Omaha. The Clarinda, built in 1909, was named for Welch's hometown, and The Page, built in 1914, for his home county.

The apartments were designed as spacious seven room units with two bathrooms, and each of the three story buildings contained six units.

The white concrete columns and decorative cast window detailing was fabricated at the Welch Sash and Door Co. in Clarinda and transported to Omaha by train.

Shortly after completion of The Page, the Welches moved to Omaha. Many prominent members of the business and civic community once lived in these fine apartments.

They were restored in 1977.

3027 Farnam St. and 305-311 Turner Blvd.
BUILT: 1909 (Clarinda); 1914 (Page)
BUILDER: *William W. Welch*
STYLE: *Georgian Revival/Classical Revival*

First Unitarian Church of Omaha

1910 – 1919

Let us think, as we lay stone upon stone,
that a time is to come when those stones will be held sacred...

Listed on the National Register of Historic Places

ERECTED FOR THE CITY NATIONAL BANK, this was Omaha's first skyscraper. At 16 stories, it signaled a new era in the commercial development of the city. Built on a riveted steel skeleton, a specialty of the Chicago architects Holabird and Roach, the façade is buff brick with a terra cotta cornice and granite detailing.

The design allowed for high-density office use in that none of the interior walls were needed for structural support. The plan allowed maximum flexibility, and easily met the tenants' needs.

Even the plumbing layout was made efficient by stacking the sanitary units.

Vacant for several years, K. C. Knudson purchased the building in 1985 and completely renovated it to provide commercial space, as well as 130 residential apartments. The lobby was restored with marble floors, wood paneling and crystal chandeliers.

405 S. 16th St.
BUILT: 1910
ARCHITECT: *Holabird and Roche*
STYLE: *Italianate/Classical*

Designated Omaha Landmark: June 18, 1985   *Listed on the National Register of Historic Places*

THE KENNEDY BUILDING, often referred to as Union Outfitting, is a classic local adaptation of Louis Sullivan's Chicago School style. This innovation created unity in a multi-storied structure by dividing the façade into a three-part scheme of base, shaft and capital – suggesting a classical column. During the first three decades of the 20th century, this was a dominant feature in commercial building design.

The Kennedy Investment Co. constructed the building in 1910 for $100,000 to use as a showroom/warehouse. It is seven stories plus basement, and incorporates both load-bearing masonry walls and independent steel columns.

The first two floors had large display windows suitable for showrooms. Floors three through seven were also designed with an open floor plan, allowing various uses. Exterior construction was brick with alternating bands of terra cotta used to delineate the various levels. The structure is crowned at the roofline by an elaborate projecting galvanized sheet iron cornice that is a distinctive aspect of the façade.

The building was leased first to the People's Furniture and Carpet Co. In 1924, the Union Outfitting Co. occupied the building and remained for more than 60 years.

There have been several remodelings, the most extensive in 1936. In the 1980s, the structure was renovated again, this time for use as residential apartments. Throughout the years, the integrity of the original façade has been well preserved.

1517 Jackson St.
BUILT: 1910
ARCHITECT: *Fisher and Lawrie*
STYLE: *Commercial*

Listed on the National Register of Historic Places

IN 1908, the Douglas County Commissioners passed a resolution that called for a new courthouse. A subsequent vote on a bond issue was successful, and Omaha architect John Latenser Sr. was engaged to provide the design for a structure not to exceed $1 million in cost.

Construction began in the spring of 1909, and the structure was completed on Oct. 1, 1912. It is one of Latenser's most significant buildings, and an important work of public architecture. The architect's design is constructed on a steel frame with walls of Bedford limestone on a granite base.

The atrium rises 110 feet, and features a double skylight and dome with large mural panels that convey the beauty of the original interior. The floors are terrazzo and much of the original fine marble wainscotting on the walls and stairways remains.

During a riot in 1919, the building was set afire and the interior sustained much damage. In addition, numerous alterations through the years have tended to obscure some of the original interior design.

Today, the building continues in use for courts and offices and the façade retains its original appearance and historic integrity.

17th and Farnam Streets
BUILT: 1912
ARCHITECT: *John Latenser Sr.*
STYLE: *French Renaissance Revival*

Designated Omaha Landmark: Jan. 13, 1998

Listed on the National Register of Historic Places

THIS STRUCTURE with its central portico, pilasters, Palladian window and detailed cornice is one of the best examples of Neoclassical Revival style architecture as applied to an educational building in Omaha. After a shift from the Richardson Romanesque style of the late 19th century, this classical design form gained immediate and vast popularity.

Originally constructed in 1910 as the Franklin School, an addition to increase classroom space occurred in 1916. The building is primarily brick, and utilizes a decorative limestone trim on the exterior façade. The name of the school was changed to Robbins in 1928 to memorialize two heroic Omaha lads. The boys had run into their burning home to rescue their invalid mother, resulting in the death of one of them in the fire. The other was killed a year later in a sledding accident.

Robbins School closed in 1994, and in the late 1990s was totally renovated for use as a residential apartment building. The elegant and historic façade has been retained.

4302 S. 39th Ave.
BUILT: 1910
ARCHITECT: *Unknown*
STYLE: *Neoclassical Revival*

Designated Omaha Landmark: Sept. 18, 1984

Listed on the National Register of Historic Places

CONSTRUCTED PRIMARILY of red brick, the two-story structure incorporates many decorative elements including a stately main entrance flanked by columns and a lantern cupola on the roof.

The school was named for Edward A. Rosewater, founder, editor and publisher of the *Omaha Bee News*. A Czech immigrant, he organized the newspaper in 1871, and used its influence to establish a strong base of power in the community.

Always interested in education, Rosewater was one of the initial organizers of the Omaha School District and the local Board of Education. He died in 1906.

After the school closed, the building was renovated in 1985 for use as residential apartments. Although many interior changes were necessary, the classical and historic façade has been retained.

3764 S. 13th St.
BUILT: 1910
ARCHITECT: *Frederick W. Clarke*
STYLE: *Second Renaissance Revival*

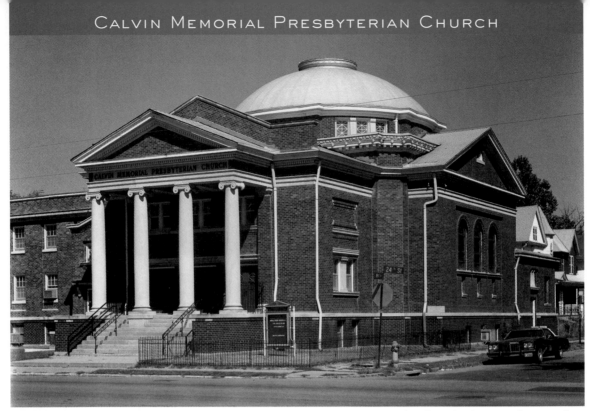

Designated Omaha Landmark: Jan. 22, 1985

Listed on the National Register of Historic Places

THIS EXCELLENT EXAMPLE of Neoclassical Revival styling was built in 1910. The structure is distinguished by a large central dome covering the main auditorium and a grand main façade exhibiting a triangular pediment supported by four Doric columns.

Originally constructed to serve the North Presbyterian Church congregation, in 1954 Calvin Memorial Presbyterian Church established an integrated congregation and took ownership. Today Church of Jesus Christ – Whole Truth holds services in the building and the church continues to serve as an important landmark in the north Omaha community.

3105 N. 24th St.
BUILT: 1910
ARCHITECT: *Frederick A. Henninger*
STYLE: *Neoclassical Revival*

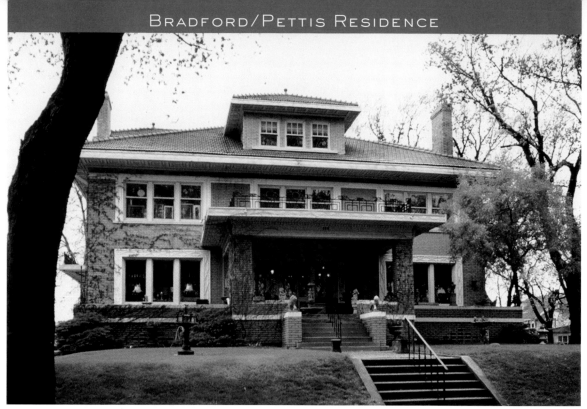

Designated Omaha Landmark: Feb. 26, 1980　　*Listed on the National Register of Historic Places*

JOHN MCDONALD designed this large, modified Prairie School style residence for Dana C. and Savilla Bradford. Bradford was the owner of Bradford-Kennedy Lumber Co., one of the largest wholesale lumber dealers in the country prior to World War I.

Although of substantial proportion, the exterior design is somewhat restrained. The overhanging eves and strong horizontal planes are distinctive Prairie School features. The construction material is primarily brick and the roof is red clay tile.

The spacious interior contains many distinctive design elements, including leaded glass windows, decorative tile fireplaces and inlaid wood.

After the death of Bradford in 1923, his widow married Edward F. Pettis. Pettis, who at that time was secretary-treasurer and director of the J. L. Brandeis and Sons store, was instrumental in the founding of the College World Series.

In 1964, the house was acquired by Jack and Louis Drew, and converted for use as a gallery to accommodate their art and antiques business.

Presently used as a Montessori school, the exterior remains mostly original. There have been some interior modifications.

404 S. 39th St.
BUILT: 1910
ARCHITECT: *John McDonald*
STYLE: *Prairie School*

In 1903, the First Church of Christ Scientist purchased a building site at 24th Street and St. Mary's Avenue. Funds were raised, and in time, local architect Frederick W. Clarke was commissioned to provide a building plan. The cornerstone of the new building was laid Oct. 6, 1909.

This impressive classically styled building was built at an initial cost of $70,000. It is constructed of buff colored brick with an extensive use of Bedford limestone. Two large columns flank the high, rounded arch on the main façade. The dome was originally covered with red clay Spanish tile. Large stained glass windows are set into the east and west façadess.

The sanctuary and a balcony can seat 1200. Floors are of hard maple, but include great use of inlaid mosaic tile in the lobby area. All interior woodwork is solid oak, including the bench seats. A most outstanding design feature is an expansive dome, with a stained glass center covers the main auditorium. It has surrounding curves that blend into four large arches. Sidelights are also stained glass.

First services were held on Sept. 3, 1911, although the official dedication did not take place until Feb. 1, 1914. As the needs of the congregation changed, the building was sold in 1997 and the church is now occupied by another congregation.

2242 St. Mary's Ave.
BUILT: 1911
ARCHITECT: *Frederick W. Clarke*
STYLE: *Classical Revival/Adam*

THE FOREST LAWN MEMORIAL PARK has existed since 1885. Located in northeast Omaha, it encompasses approximately 320 acres. The chapel at Forest Lawn is a prominent feature of this location and a noteworthy example of Classical Revival architecture.

After reviewing many similar structures throughout the country, architect John McDonald produced this pleasing design in 1911. The Masonic Grand Lodge of Nebraska laid the cornerstone Dec. 27, 1911.

The interior was designed and installed by J. and R. Lamb of New York. The finest materials of mosaic, Colorado-Yule marble, and bronze were used and it required more than two years to complete the designs prior to their installation.

Mosaic panels containing gold ornamentation and mother-of-pearl accent the walls and ceilings using naturalistic designs. The floor is a decorative combination of tile and marble. Specially designed marble furniture and marble lights enrich the interior. Doors and window frames are bronze and the roof is covered with green clay tile.

The exterior measuring 40′ x 64′ is constructed of St. Cloud granite. Façades are essentially symmetrical, each set off with four columns over a raised pediment. On the lower level is located a columbarium and receiving vault.

Forest Lawn Memorial Park
7909 Mormon Bridge Road
BUILT: 1911
ARCHITECT: *John McDonald*
STYLE: *Classical Revival*

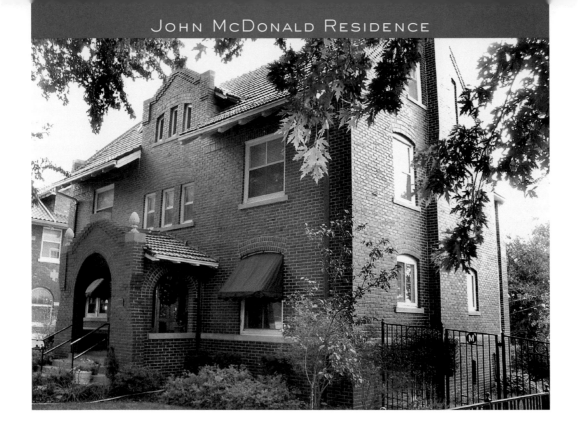

John McDonald designed this home for himself and wife, Martha. Located in the Cathedral neighborhood, the house is of a modest scale. However, the plan demonstrates many elegant, yet restrained, design features.

The house is two and one-half stories and is constructed in red brick. The roof is green clay tile. McDonald included a distinctive front entry, composed of a small pavilion and parapet with a gable roof and central rounded arch. The exterior exhibits a limited use of limestone trim for accents.

The interior is finished with exotic woods, including an extensive use of mahogany. This rich wood is used as paneling throughout the public rooms and central hallway and also in the beamed ceilings in the living and dining rooms. A fireplace graces the master bedroom.

John McDonald lived here until his passing in 1956. Throughout its history, the home has had only three owners, and therefore retains almost all of its original form and design.

515 N. 38th St.
BUILT: 1911
ARCHITECT: *John McDonald*
STYLE: *Jacobethan Revival*

FLATIRON HOTEL

Listed on the National Register of Historic Places

DUE TO THE IRREGULAR shaped triangular lot, formed by the convergence of Howard Street and St. Mary's Avenue, the Flatiron building has a most distinctive design and remains a city landmark. Architect George B. Prinz drew on the original Flatiron Building in New York City in his design for developers Henry Payne and Ralph Slater.

The four-story building is unique in Omaha. The symmetrical façade is placed along St. Mary's Avenue, with a slightly projecting main entrance. A circular tower, placed at the point of the triangle is highlighted by decorative brickwork. Limestone trim is used to accent the window arches and sills, and the brown brick exterior contains many decorative elements.

Originally constructed for use as commercial and office space, this unusual structure served as a hotel for many years. The building has been renovated for offices and a restaurant and continues to add much visual interest to downtown Omaha.

1722 St. Mary's Ave.
BUILT: 1912
ARCHITECT: *George B. Prinz*
STYLE: *Georgian Revival*

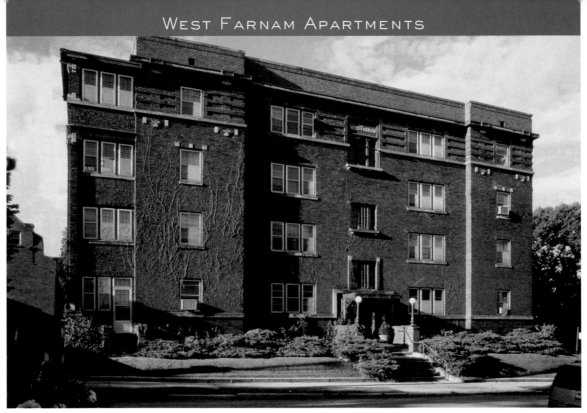

Designated Omaha Landmark: Sept. 26, 1979

THE WEST FARNAM BUILDING was the earliest luxury apartment built in Omaha. It was constructed for $30,000 and designed by Omaha architect Frederick A. Henninger.

The structure has four levels, over a raised basement. It is brown brick with load-bearing walls, and is crowned by a plain brick parapet wall. The linear and symmetrical façade is quite simple and there is limited use of limestone trim. Subtle prairie style brick ornamentation strengthens the overall horizontal design elements.

Prairie style columns and sidelights flank the main entrance. Two low brick walls project outward, providing support for twin cast iron entry lights. Above the central entrance is a leaded, clear glass, three-part window from which two wood columns rise and support a plaque inscribed with the West Farnam name.

The building contains eight apartments, of identical size and configuration. The ceilings are 10 feet in height and all floors and interior woodwork are quartersawn oak. When built amenities included an electric elevator, spacious floor plan, and a flowering garden. The 11 steam-heated garages were constructed in 1920 for $5,000.

Originally Dr. Jesse McMullen, an Omaha dentist, owned the building. He resided at the West Farnam in apartment #1.

There have been few alterations to these large luxury apartments. They are currently fully occupied and remain in good condition.

3817 Dewey Ave.
BUILT: 1912
ARCHITECT: *Frederick A. Henninger*
STYLE: *Commercial/Prairie School*

THIS STATELY RESIDENCE was built for Minnie Storz Higgins as a wedding gift from her father, Omaha brewer, Gottlieb Storz.

Constructed of brick, the house features exterior detailing finished in limestone. The symmetrical façade has a porte-cochere on the south side balanced by a sun porch on the north. Matching parapets and second floor oriel windows are placed above the central arched entry. Other exterior features include decorative overhanging eaves, red clay tile roof, and brick balustrades at both the front porch and second floor roof terraces. Mahogany is used extensively for the interior, as well as decorative iron work and stained glass windows.

Mrs. Higgins was a well-known hostess, and entertained enthusiastically. After her death in 1971, the home was purchased by the Boetel Co. and converted to office use.

Used today as an event venue, the Renaissance welcomes guests as it once did during the residency of Minnie Storz Higgins.

401 S. 39th St.
BUILT: 1913
ARCHITECT: *H. A. Raapke*
STYLE: *Jacobethan Revival*

ALTHOUGH THE DESIGN of this house is characteristic of the Georgian Revival style, it exhibits numerous eclectic features. Designed by Omaha architect George B. Prinz, it was built in 1914 for Omaha businessman Arthur Metz. Metz was one of four brothers who owned and operated Metz Brothers Brewing Co. Prior to prohibition, their company was one of the largest and most successful breweries in Omaha.

Somewhat more modest than other homes in the prestigious Gold Coast area, it is constructed of gray brick and trimmed with limestone. The understated detailing imparts an image of substance and refinement that elevates the overall design. This home is an excellent example of the residences constructed in the early part of the 20th century by successful business and community leaders as a statement of their position in society.

Although the building has been divided into apartment units, the façade of the Metz home retrains great integrity.

3625 Dewey Ave.
BUILT: 1914
ARCHITECT: *George B. Prinz*
STYLE: *Georgian Revival*

THIS BUILDING, now known as the Omaha Scottish Rite Masonic Center, is an important landmark in downtown Omaha. First chartered in 1885, the Omaha Valley of Scottish Rite has occupied a prominent place in the community for decades.

Groundbreaking occurred at 20th and Douglas Streets June 5, 1912, and the cornerstone was laid on Oct. 2, 1912.

Built on a steel frame, the main exterior façades are entirely of Bedford limestone. Two large Ionic limestone columns rise the entire three-story height of the building and frame the strong portico that defines the former front entrance on Douglas Street. The entire cost of the original structure was $200,000.

The building has more than 47,000 square feet of space on four floors and an attic. The first level contains offices, a dining room, museum and kitchen. The second level has a lounge, meeting rooms, and a large ball-room. The third level has a remarkable 400-seat proscenium theater with a 46-foot stage opening, a full-height stage house, and numerous historical painted theatrical backdrops. The organ was installed in 1926 and has 25 ranks making it one of the largest organs in Omaha.

The rest of the third floor contains ceremonial rooms and the fourth floor houses a library and costume storage.

Fine quality oak woodwork is used throughout, in addition to marble and terrazzo.

In 1968, the original Latenser firm was engaged to renovate and develop a courtyard on the east side, which today serves as the accessible entry to the building. Recently, the entire structure has undergone an extensive restoration that was accomplished in an elegant and historically accurate manner.

202 S. 20th St.
BUILT: 1914
ARCHITECT: *John Latenser Sr.*
STYLE: *Neoclassical Revival*

LOUIS C. NASH RESIDENCE

THIS SUBSTANTIAL HOME WAS BUILT for Louis C. Nash, an executive of the Burgess-Nash Department store.

The house has a total of 32 rooms, with 10 bedrooms and seven bathrooms. Constructed with load-bearing mansonry walls it has a side gabled red clay tile roof. Prominent parapeted cross gables and two large chimneys project above the roofline. The brick is set in English bond pattern.

Bedford stone surrounds the windows, and limestone decorates the parapets and quoins. An immense two-story bay window projects from the central cross gable creating a frame for the main entry. A porte-cochere is located along the west façade.

Interior features include an impressive entry hall, with double staircase and quartersawn oak paneling. On second floor, the main bedroom suites have a series of inter-connecting doors. The interior fixtures throughout the house are of the highest quality. A ballroom is located on the third floor, as well as large storage rooms and servants living quarters.

The Nash family sold the house in 1941.

3807 Burt St.
BUILT: 1914
ARCHITECT: *George B. Prinz*
STYLE: *Jacobethan Revival*

THE EMINENT NEW YORK ARCHITECT Henry Bacon designed this structure. Bacon is known for his creation of the Lincoln Memorial in Washington, D. C. and numerous other public and private buildings and memorials.

The N. P. Dodge Co., original owners of Westlawn Cemetery, provided the building site to the Nebraska Mausoleum Co. The structure, costing in excess of $460,000, was built between 1913 and 1915 and the mausoleum was formally dedicated Sept. 12, 1915. A noteworthy aspect of construction of the mausoleum is that it is also made from the same Colorado-Yule Marble as the Lincoln Memorial. Constructed of solid marble blocks throughout, the interior is a finer quality, highly polished Golden Vein marble.

The overall structure is 83.5′ x 148′, rendered in stylized Doric pilasters and a classic Greek temple

pediment. On the south side of the building is a 12′ x 18′ receiving vault. The interior contains space for 650 crypts, as well as niches for 300 urns in columbaria.

Within the main façade, an elegant pediment surmounts an entry with artistic double doors of solid bronze. Deeply set windows of green stained glass relieve the classic exterior surfaces of the walls. The interior contains a spacious chapel with carved marble pulpit and several private memorial rooms.

This is the first community mausoleum erected in Nebraska. The builders considered a plan to replicate the design in other locations, however this was not accomplished. In 1937, the mausoleum became non-participatory and Westlawn-Hillcrest assumed management.

Westlawn-Hillcrest Memorial Park
57th and Center Streets
BUILT: 1915
ARCHITECT: *Henry Bacon*
STYLE: *Classic Revival/Greco-Roman Temple*

CHARLES E. METZ RESIDENCE

THIS IMPRESSIVE GOLD COAST MANSION was built for Charles E. Metz, an owner of the Metz Brewing Co. Constructed on a grand and elegant scale, the home cost $175,000 in 1915. It is a fine example of the Georgian Revival style, which was a preferred design of wealthy families at the time.

The house is solid masonry construction with extensive use of Bedford limestone trim and detailing throughout. Two pairs of limestone Corinthian columns flank the elegant front entrance. Windows are asymmetrical, diminishing in size from first through third floors and balustrade sills and entablatures ornament the first floor windows. A massive cornice crowns the structure.

Within the house, there is extensive use of hand-carved walnut paneling in the main hall and stairway. The dining room walls are paneled, with hand-tooled leather borders. A solarium contains a marble fountain, and is dominated by a large Palladian window.

Over the years, the first and second floor and basement have undergone some modifications. The northwest corner of the house is attached to a carriage house that is now used as a garage.

The Phi Chi Fraternity of the University of Nebraska Medical Center has owned and occupied the house for many years.

3708 Dewey Ave.
BUILT: 1915
ARCHITECT: *George B. Prinz*
STYLE: *Georgian Revival*

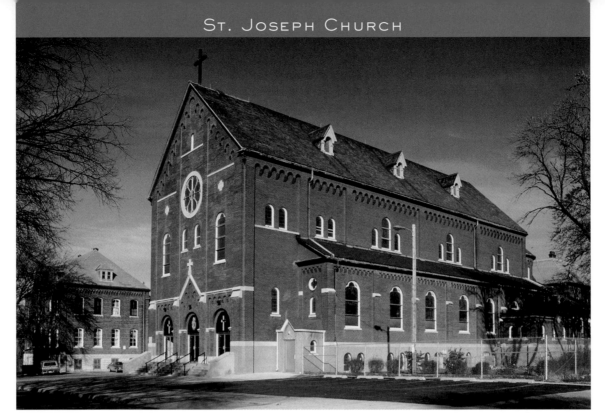

Designated Omaha Landmark: Feb. 11, 1986 *Listed on the National Register of Historic Places*

ESTABLISHED AS OMAHA'S second German speaking parish in 1886, St. Joseph's became an important center for one of the largest immigrant groups in the city. It is a prime example of the rich cultural and ethnic heritage that played an important role in the development of Omaha.

The Franciscan Fathers, a missionary order working with German and Polish speaking communities throughout Nebraska, developed the parish and in 1915 drew upon the skill of one of their members, architect Brother Leonard Darscheidt. An important example of Romanesque Revival design, the church is constructed primarily of brick with limestone trim.

The church is part of a parish complex and remains under the administration of the Franciscan Fathers today. It continues to serve the expanded local community, while drawing on the original traditions and cultural heritage of the parish.

1730 S. 16th St.
BUILT: 1915
ARCHITECT: *Brother Leonard Darscheidt*
STYLE: *German Romanesque Revival*

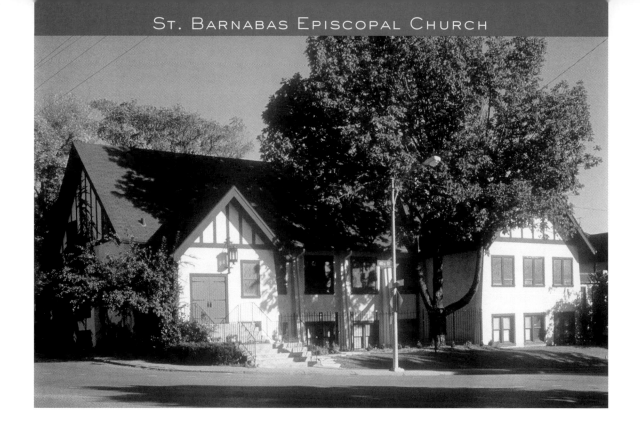

THE PARISH OF ST. BARNABAS was organized May 3, 1869, and was sponsored by Trinity Cathedral.

The new parish initially located in a small wooden structure near 9th and Douglas Streets. This building was later moved to 14th and Cass Streets. In 1870, they moved again to 19th and California Streets. The congregation remained there until 1913, when land was purchased at 40th and Davenport Streets as a setting for the present church.

Of timber and stucco construction, the appearance and configuration of the church built on this site resembles the style of English Herefordshire architecture. The sanctuary was extended in 1920 to provide additional space.

Magnificent stained glass windows surround the nave and are from the famous studio of C. E. Kemp. The C. T. Kountze family provided the windows to the church in the 1920s. Additional windows by Ernest Lakeman were installed in 1935.

The interior contains many significant works of ecclesiastical art. Included are terra cotta reliefs from Italy and magnificent woodcarvings from Oberammergau, Germany. A side chapel also contains many interesting objects. A respectful parish has maintained the church in very good condition.

129 N. 40th St.
BUILT: 1915
ARCHITECT: *Charles M. Nye*
STYLE: *English Country Tudor Revival*

SANFORD HOTEL/CONANT APARTMENTS

Designated Omaha Landmark: Feb. 26, 1985   *Listed on the National Register of Historic Places*

DR. HAROLD GIFFORD SR., an internationally known ophthalmologist and prominent philanthropist, built the Sanford Hotel between 1916 and 1917. It is an adaptation of the then new Chicago School style of commercial architecture. Dr. Gifford built the hotel as an investment property, and in the early 1920s the hotel was leased to Harley Conant, who named it after himself in 1939, and operated it until 1950.

Built on a steel frame, the construction material is brick and concrete. The façade incorporates the design concept of a column like scheme demonstrating a base, shaft, and capitol to achieve an overall unifying effect.

The Conant remained an operational 45,000 square foot hotel until 1985. At that time, the building was renovated for use as 53 residential apartment units. The first floor was redeveloped to provide space for commercial tenants.

The original façade remains intact and the building is an attractive feature in the downtown scene.

1913 Farnam St.
BUILT: 1916
ARCHITECT: *John Latenser Sr.*
STYLE: *Chicago School/Commercial*

DRAKE COURT AND DARTMORE APARTMENTS

Designated Omaha Landmark: Dec. 19, 1978 *Listed on the National Register of Historic Places*

THIS LARGE COMPLEX of residential apartment units was constructed between 1916 and 1919. The buildings were designed, financed, and constructed by the Drake Realty Construction Co., owned by William and George Drake. The buildings contained 216 units. At the time, the Drake Co. was Omaha's largest developer of apartments, and by 1925 controlled more than 1,000 residential units. However, when the economic climate changed, Drake and his company were eventually forced into bankruptcy.

The Drake Court and Dartmore Apartments are constructed of brick and reinforced concrete. Extensive use of decorative terra cotta ornamentation lends elegance to the exterior façadess. Many Prairie School features are also incorporated.

The complex was designed and developed to provide convenient, stylish residential units for professional people working in the near downtown Omaha area. They were grouped around an attractive courtyard, and were situated within easy walking distance from the local business district.

In 2003, NuStyle Development Corporation completed a $14.3 million renovation of the buildings creating 138 apartments located in 14 buildings all connected by a beautifully renovated historic courtyard. The renovation was part of a city and neighborhood redevelopment initiative for the area.

20th to 23rd Streets, at Jones Street
BUILT: 1916
ARCHITECT AND BUILDER: *William B. Drake*
STYLE: *Georgian Revival*

GEORGE T. FORSTER RESIDENCE

THE FORSTER RESIDENCE is considered the only true rendering of residential Prairie School architecture in Omaha. After accepting a position at the Hayden Brothers Department Store, George Forster, a native of Chicago, and his wife settled in Omaha. To design their new home, Forster selected a Chicago architect, Louis Bouchard, who was a student of Frank Lloyd Wright.

Constructed in 1916, the house exhibits all of the characteristic features of Prairie School design. The architect solved the placement problem of the narrow urban lot by projecting the building toward the street and positioning the long elevation perpendicular to the front lot line. Forster resided in this house until his death in 1957.

Today, the house retains many of its original decorative features that augment this distinctive style in architecture.

3712 Davenport St.
BUILT: 1916
ARCHITECT: *Louis Bouchard*
STYLE: *Prairie School*

BLACKSTONE HOTEL

Designated Omaha Landmark: April 12, 1983

Listed on the National Register of Historic Places

WHEN BUILT, the Blackstone Hotel was designed as a family or residential hotel that was far removed from the central business district and was situated in the prestigious Gold Coast neighborhood.

The Bankers Realty Investment Co. built the Blackstone utilizing a frame of structural steel and supported it with 412 concrete piers. The exterior is brick, with an abundant use of terra cotta detailing on the façade.

Although some single rooms were available, the hotel was composed primarily of large six to eight room combination suites. In addition, it included sets of four glass sunrooms on each level, and three rooftop gardens located off the grand ballroom. The interior was an eclectic mixture of elegant appointments, with numerous ornate furnishings, a crystal chandelier and a marble grand staircase.

Due to a declining economy, the hotel was sold in 1920 to Charles Schimmel of the Schimmel Hotel Co. Under the direction of Charles and Mary Schimmel, the Blackstone became one of the most successful elegant small hotels in the country for almost 50 years.

In 1968, the Radisson Hotel Corporation of Minneapolis purchased the Blackstone and continued to operate the hotel until it was finally closed in July 1976. Subsequently, the structure was sold and redeveloped into the Blackstone Center as office space. It continues to be used as an office building today. The beautiful and artistic original façade has been well maintained.

302 S. 36th St.
BUILT: 1916
ARCHITECT: *Bankers Realty Investment Co.,*
W. V. Kernan
STYLE: *Second Renaissance Revival*

Designated Omaha Landmark: Feb. 13, 1979   *Listed on the National Register of Historic Places*

THE CONGREGATION, organized in Omaha in 1868, built its first church at 17th and Cass Streets in 1871. In 1913 the property was sold to the German American Society, and in January 1917 the group developed plans to construct a new church at 31st and Harney Streets.

This structure is an unusually fine example of Colonial Revival architecture. An elegant double door entrance is centered on the main façade, above which is a circular fanlight exhibiting delicate detail. Round arched windows flank the entrance. Five rounded, arched windows and two oculi punctuate each side wall. Largely constructed in Flemish bond of red brick, a copper dome caps a tall central steeple. The interior is an accurate representation of a classic New England house of worship from the 18th century.

Former President William Howard Taft officiated at the laying of the cornerstone on Oct. 19, 1917, and the building was officially dedicated Sept. 29, 1918.

A one-story addition at the northwest corner was constructed in 1952, to provide educational space. Omaha architect Noel Wallace designed it respecting the scale and materials of the original structure.

3114 Harney St.
BUILT: 1917
ARCHITECT: *John and Alan McDonald*
STYLE: *Georgian Colonial Revival*

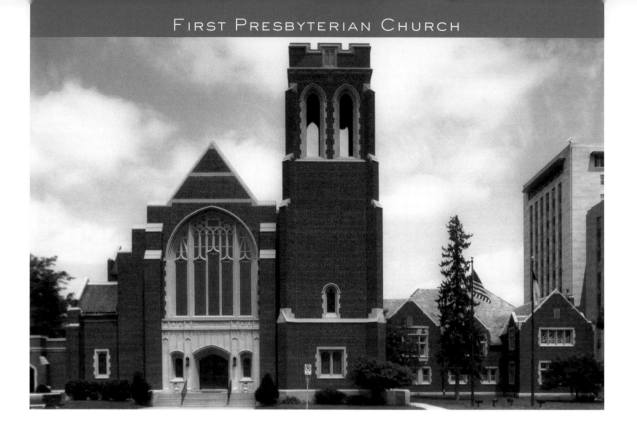

FIRST PRESBYTERIAN CHURCH

ORGANIZED IN OMAHA IN 1856, the Presbyterians erected a significant building at 17th and Dodge Streets in 1866. In 1915, the site was sold and the church relocated to 34th and Farnam Streets.

Enthusiastic churchwomen raised over $29,000, which when combined with the proceeds from the sale of the Dodge Street property, allowed construction of the new church.

Omaha architect George B. Prinz was commissioned in 1915 to design the building and selected the Collegiate Gothic style. The new facility was dedicated March 11, 1917. It is constructed of red brick with extensive use on both the exterior and interior of Bedford limestone trim. The substructure is reinforced concrete.

The interior is highlighted with a number of magnificent stained glass windows. All of the woodwork is quartersawn oak.

A two-story Memorial Building was added to the west side of the church in 1929 and is attached to the main structure by an attractive cloistered walkway.

The tall distinctive tower contains a bell carillon. At the time of its construction, this edifice was considered one of the finest church buildings in Omaha.

216 S. 34th St.
BUILT: 1917
ARCHITECT: *George B. Prinz*
STYLE: *Collegiate Gothic*

Located in a District that is Listed on the National Register of Historic Places

THIS SUBSTANTIAL HOME is one of the best examples of the work of architect F. A. Henninger Sr. It was designed for Otto H. Barmettler, who came to Omaha from Davenport, Iowa, with the American Biscuit Co. The house cost $30,000 to construct, has 23 rooms, and is two and one-half stories high.

Originally built of beige brick the house is capped with a red clay French tile roof. The exterior exhibits a large central dormer flanked by segmental arched dormers, enclosed eves, and a symmetrical façade. Roman Doric columns frame pavilions of multi-paned floor to ceiling windows. The third floor contains a large ballroom.

The Barmettler family sold the house in 1940. In 1954, Duschesne Academy purchased it to use for student housing. The present owners have renovated and restored this elegant and historic home.

622 N. 38th St.
BUILT: 1917
ARCHITECT: *Frederick A. Henninger Sr.*
STYLE: *Second Renaissance Revival*

Listed on the National Register of Historic Places

ONE OF OMAHA's earliest financial institutions, First National Bank, traces its origins to the Kountze Brothers Banking House which began operation in December 1857. In 1863, it was reorganized under the national banking laws, and given a charter by the Federal Government.

Great changes took place in the development of the downtown Omaha financial and commercial district in the first two decades of the 20th century. Several business owners looked to Chicago architects to provide designs for their projects, including the First National Bank. This 14-story building was designed by Graham, Burnham and Co. and completed in 1917.

The building, constructed with a distinctive "U" opening in the façade, gives the impression of towers rising above the fourth level. Built with structural steel, it is clad in buff colored brick with terra cotta and granite trim. Originally the first floor was used for shops and a lobby. The second and third stories that are tied together by two-story pilasters and wall cornices were home to the bank offices.

The First National Bank occupied the building until the 1970s. In 1987, the structure was renovated by three Minneapolis/St. Paul investors for use as residential apartments. There have been few exterior alterations to the original structure.

16th and Farnam Streets
BUILT: 1917
ARCHITECT: *Graham, Burnham and Co.*
STYLE: *Late Renaissance Revival*

PARK SCHOOL

Designated Omaha Landmark: June 12, 1990   *Listed on the National Register of Historic Places*

PARK SCHOOL is one of a number of schools designed by architect Thomas R. Kimball. The name was derived from its proximity to Hanscom Park.

The basic structure is masonry, on a frame of reinforced concrete. Limestone trim is used for ornamentation on the principal elevations. When constructed in 1918, it contained 18 rooms.

Overall the design is quite restrained and straightforward. The footprint is "U," shaped and consists of two stories over an elevated basement. The roof is flat and concealed by a decorative shaped parapet.

In construction, attempts were made to reduce costs, and several design features, such as a gymnasium and library were eliminated. The interior finishing is rather plain, with maple flooring, smooth plaster walls, and painted rather than finished wood doors. All of this is reflective of the constraints of construction undertaken during World War I. The entire cost of the school was $142,000.

After the school was closed, the Omaha Public School district sold it in 1988. Subsequently, the building was renovated and remodeled for use as residential apartment units.

The historic and architectural integrity of the structure has been well maintained.

1320 S. 29th St.
BUILT: 1918
ARCHITECT: *Thomas R. Kimball*
STYLE: *Collegiate Gothic*

ST. REGIS APARTMENTS

PLANS WERE ACCEPTED for this luxury apartment building located in the Gold Coast in October 1916, and construction started soon afterward. Cost of construction was approximately $200,000 and the first tenants arrived in 1919.

Built on reinforced steel framework, all exterior construction is brick, with a limited use of decorative limestone and terra cotta. A central section is flanked by two projecting wings on the north and south and presents a symmetrical appearance. A small courtyard originally contained a fountain and reflecting pool, within an attractively landscaped garden setting.

The ground floor featured four two-bedroom apartments, a café and store, laundry area, servant's parlor, and one-room servant's quarters. The north and south wings contained three residence floors. Above that, each level had two 10-room residential suites. The central section had four levels above the ground floor, which contained more modest two-bedroom apartments.

With changing residential requirements over the years, all of the large suites have been divided and additional garages were constructed in 1965. The elegant structure continues to add charm and dignity to the neighborhood. The building is very well maintained and remains in excellent condition.

617 S. 37th St.
BUILT: 1919
ARCHITECT: *Bankers Realty Investment Co.*
STYLE: *Eclectic*

Designated Omaha Landmark: July 14, 1981   *Listed on the National Register of Historic Places*

THIS IS THE MOST significant existing example of Commercial architectural style executed by the McDonald firm and incorporates many Georgian Colonial Revival elements as well.

Omaha businessmen John W. and Lem H. Hill hired Vaughn Construction Co. to build the Hill Hotel for $250,000.

The structure is 14 stories tall and originally contained 140 rooms. The frame is cast concrete, clad in brown brick. The structure is 160 feet high, and is capped by its most distinctive design feature, a widely projecting and heavily bracketed copper-clad cornice. With considerable use of limestone trim, the exterior façade is notable for its association with the Chicago School concept of skyscraper design. The carefully detailed elevations denote an advance in local design thinking.

Many of the interior features have been altered, and after serving as a hotel for more than 60 years, the building was converted into residential apartments in the 1980s.

505 S. 16th St.
BUILT: 1919
ARCHITECT: *John and Alan McDonald*
STYLE: *Georgian Colonial Revival/Commercial*

Aquila Court

1920 - 1954

Men will say as they look upon the labor and wrought substance from them
'See! This our fathers did for us.'

St. John's A.M.E. Church

Designated Omaha Landmark: Dec. 19, 1978　　　　*Listed on the National Register of Historic Places*

THIS CHURCH IS one of Omaha's few mature examples of Prairie School architecture as developed and conceived by Frank Lloyd Wright.

Construction began in 1921 and in 1923 the raised basement and stair towers at the northeast and southeast corner were completed. Church members agreed that the building would go forward only as funds became available. Therefore, services continued to be held in the basement of the partially completed church for 21 years.

The building is constructed in brick with concrete trim. The foundation is granite and a continuous stone band defines the two levels. Deep sash windows provide light to the basement area.

The broad, flat roof emphasizes the horizontal plane. Steel columns covered in brick support the roof, which is poured concrete. Many linear design features are also found in the interior. In keeping with the original plan, the main auditorium was completed in 1947. Additional space was obtained through the placement of five meeting rooms east of the auditorium in 1956.

2402 N. 22nd St.
BUILT: 1923
ARCHITECT: *Frederick S. Stott*
STYLE: *Prairie School*

Listed on the National Register of Historic Places

THIS SIX-STORY BUILDING is constructed with reinforced concrete faced in brick and is trimmed with limestone. The father and son McDonald firm designed it in 1919.

Constructed between 1920 and 1922, these offices were built as the headquarters for the central region of the Standard Oil Co. At the time, this was one of Omaha's taller buildings.

Of special interest is the cornice ornamentation, soffits, and fascia, which are of formed metal. The original design of the rooms and hallways allowed for spacious open areas in conjunction with smaller offices and working spaces.

The lobby, vestibule, and vaulted ceiling are marble, which has been obscured by the installation of acoustic tile to allow for the addition of ductwork for air-conditioning.

The main structure of the building remains unchanged.

500 S. 18th St.
BUILT: 1922
ARCHITECT: *John and Alan McDonald*
STYLE: *Chicago School/Commercial*

Listed on the National Register of Historic Places

THIS EXCEPTIONAL STRUCTURE is the result of a very productive architect/client relationship by the Chicago firm of Holabird and Roach. Built for Chicago capitalists and developers Charles and Raymond Cook, and named for their father, the building is a significant structure as it represents a new concept in multi-purpose buildings.

Raymond Cook, the partner most involved in its development, insisted that an interior courtyard be included, reminiscent of an Italian garden he liked in Chicago. Landscape gardening was his hobby, and he personally supervised the development of the court.

Built in a "U" shape on a structural steel frame, the focus is the interior court, the facing walls of which are red brick. The façades on Howard Street and 16th Street rise to four stories and are faced with Bedford limestone.

The south wing includes court-level commercial space, with studio apartments above. The apartments were two-story units with a bedroom balcony and living room space, which overlooked the courtyard.

An arcade surrounded the interior court, serving as a screen against the surrounding businesses. Entering from 17th Street through an arch and colonnade, the unique and serene atmosphere resembled an Italian formal garden complete with stone paths, pools of gold fish, and numerous plants.

In 1972, the court was extensively remodeled and completely covered with split-marble slabs. Modern fountains and a large ornamental waterwheel replace the pools and canals.

Although the elegant and classical façade remains unchanged, much interior alteration has taken place. The building is now used as a hotel.

1615 Howard St.
BUILT: 1923
ARCHITECT: *Holabird and Roach*
STYLE: *Renaissance Revival/Commercial*

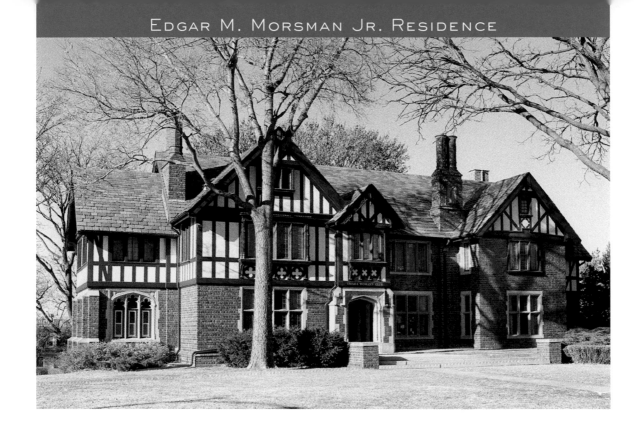

EDGAR M. MORSMAN JR. RESIDENCE

THE WORK OF OMAHA ARCHITECT Frederick A. Henninger, this substantial residence was the last great home built in the Gold Coast area.

Constructed with oversized brick, its design incorporates many Tudor elements. Imitation half-timbering with quatrefoil filling, a projected limestone entry arch, fluted chimneys, and leaded windows set in limestone frames, give added detail. The roof is steeply pitched and gables are covered with variegated slate shingles. The overall design is significant in that it includes an attached garage; the first Omaha home to incorporate this innovation.

Interior elements include hand-carved quartersawn oak woodwork and bookcases, leaded glass windows, and an elegant marble fireplace in the library.

After the death of Edgar M. Morsman in 1964, the Omaha Women's Club purchased the house and the next year it became their clubhouse. Recently, the Omaha Woman's Club sold the structure to the University of Nebraska College of Medicine for future development. In the meantime, the club continues to use it under an agreement with the college.

The structure retains almost all of its original design and appearance today.

518 S. 38th St.
BUILT: 1923
ARCHITECT: *Frederick A. Henninger*
STYLE: *Elizabethan Tudor Revival*

Designated Omaha Landmark: Sept. 9, 1980   *Listed on the National Register of Historic Places*

THE TWO-STORY BRICK STRUCTURE was designed and built for prominent businessman James C. Jewell Sr. Prior to building at this location he had operated "Jewell and Phannix," a billiard hall, at 14th and Dodge Streets.

The Jewell building originally consisted of commercial space and apartments on the first floor. Upstairs, a large public hall became the Dreamland Ballroom. The club featured big bands and jazz performances by many of the greatest jazz figures of the period.

When James Jewell Jr. took over the management of the ballroom, he refused to seek a liquor license, thereby allowing young people to also attend the jazz performances.

During 1945, the hall was used as a USO center for African American soldiers. Jewell continued operating the hall until 1965. In later years, the building was redeveloped for use as commercial and residential space. The building continues to play an important part in the North Omaha community.

2221-2225 N. 24th St.
BUILT: 1923
ARCHITECT: *Frederick A. Henninger*
STYLE: *Vernacular/Georgian Revival*

THE OMAHA HIGH SCHOOL OF COMMERCE was established in 1912 to provide technical and career-oriented training programs rather than strictly academic instruction. These courses proved very popular and soon the existing school on Leavenworth Street was not large enough.

A site was obtained between 30th and 33rd Streets and between Cuming and Burt Streets, in 1921. The architects, Frederick and Edwin Clarke, submitted their design and explained that their concept included frescoes, mosaics, tiles and sculpture which were intended to educate both the mind and the eye of the students.

Completed in 1923, the school was an imposing structure of red brick, liberally embellished with Bedford stone and terra cotta trim. Construction cost was $3.5 million. The projected enrollment was 3,000 with a faculty of 115.

As built, the school contained two large cafeterias, a huge gymnasium, and an enclosed swimming pool. The roofs of the two wing sections provided an outdoor promenade. The central section was five stories high, and the entire school contained over 400,000 square feet of space. An impressive auditorium provided seating for 2,000.

Marble, onyx and bronze decorated the interior and all woodwork was solid oak. At the time of completion, it was one of the finest structures for education in the country.

With changing neighborhood demography and declining enrollment, the high school was closed in 1984. Plans were undertaken to renovate and remodel the building for use by the Omaha Public Schools as a Teacher and Administrative Center. The extensive remodeling plan, costing approximately $10 million was completed several years later. The Administrative Center opened in the summer of 1989.

33rd and Cuming Streets
BUILT: 1923
ARCHITECT: *Frederick W. and Edwin Clarke*
STYLE: *Georgian Revival*

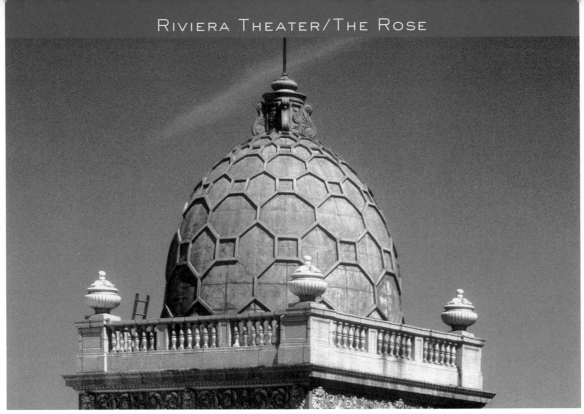

Designated Omaha Landmark: Oct. 21, 1980　　　　　　*Listed on the National Register of Historic Places*

BUILT TO RESEMBLE A MOORISH PALACE, this unique style is rarely seen in the region. The original theater was large with a seating capacity of 2,776. The visual effect of the interior was breathtaking, with rosebuds floating in fountains, goldfish swimming in aquariums, and performances under the canopy of a star-covered sky.

The exterior is no less distinctive. Constructed with a steel frame, the façade is glazed brick arranged in diamond-shaped patterns. A tower with a copper dome tops the northeast corner. Six freestanding columns, with middle-eastern ornamentation support griffin-like figures on the east elevation. This structure is an outstanding example of the "atmospheric" theater style developed especially by Chicago architect Eberson.

In 1929, due to financial losses, the theater was sold to the Paramount Co. and renamed the Paramount Theater; however, in 1957 the company vacated their lease to Creighton University. Closed for several years, in 1961 it was leased to J. S. B. Amusement Corp. and was renovated for use as a bowling alley. A year later, remodeled once again, it reopened as the Astro Theater and continued operations until June 1980.

Vacant for many years, the once elegant theater faced demolition until Rose Blumkin, founder of the Nebraska Furniture Mart, purchased it. Restored through her generosity, the Rose Blumkin Performing Arts Center, or more simply, The Rose, once again charms its patrons. This signifigant building continues to serve the community and enrich our environment.

2001 Farnam St.
BUILT: 1926
ARCHITECT: *John Eberson*
STYLE: *Moorish/Classical Revival*

Designated Omaha Landmark: June 22, 1999

Listed on the National Register of Historic Places

THIS DISTINCTIVE SOUTH OMAHA LANDMARK has been the most prominent visual element of that area since the time of its construction in 1926. It was for many years a symbol of the national role that Omaha played in the livestock and meat packing industry.

When constructed, it was the first $1 million project of Peter Kiewit and Sons construction company. George Prinz, the architect, employed medieval Romanesque details and Renaissance elements in the design of this immense building.

The use of an "H" shaped configuration provides a central circulation core and allows maximum ventilation and light to the multiple offices in each of the narrow legs. Eleven stories high, the frame of structural steel is covered by concrete, and all floors are cast concrete. Almost all of the exterior façade is dark brick, laid in decorative patterns. There is limited use of stone and terra cotta, however these materials are used at the double compound arched entry.

The main lobby is 60 feet square and two levels high. Floors two through nine provided 200 office suites for livestock commission agents as well as apartments, sleeping rooms and a cafeteria. On the 10th floor, a spacious auditorium and ballroom were situated, each two stories high.

The design of this structure is both attractive and functional. Although not lavish or costly, the interior appointments were of fine quality with much use of mahogany and oak trim.

After closing the major components of the livestock industry in Omaha, the Exchange building was vacated for a number of years.

The City of Omaha has recently turned the building over to the Nu-Style Development Co., which plans to undertake complete renovation and re-development. The future of this distinctive landmark seems bright and secure.

2900 O Plaza
BUILT: 1926
ARCHITECT: *George B. Prinz*
STYLE: *Romanesque and North Italian Renaissance Revival*

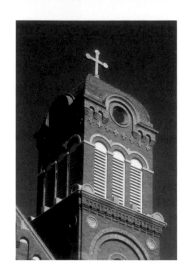

Listed on the National Register of Historic Places

THE IMMACULATE CONCEPTION parish was organized in 1895, and established as a Polish National Parish, to serve the needs of the Polish immigrants in South Omaha. This modified Romanesque Revival style church was designed by Jacob M. Nachtigall and was dedicated July 31, 1927. The design is constructed in red brick, and uses Bedford limestone as decorative trim and external accent.

The strong Romanesque form features two prominent bell towers, of identical design, that are 100 feet in height. An impressive front gable contains a beautiful rose window of jeweled stained glass set in a stone frame. The church rectory adjoins the main structure on the southwest corner.

Part of a complex that also includes a school with a large auditorium, Immaculate Conception continues to serve the community and preserve the history of its Polish heritage.

2708 S. 24th St.
BUILT: 1926
ARCHITECT: *Jacob M. Nachtigall*
STYLE: *Romanesque Revival*

Designated Omaha Landmark: April 21, 1998   *Listed on the National Register of Historic Places*

IN 1908, THE CZECH SISTERS of Notre Dame were asked by the church to come to Nebraska to teach Czech language and culture. They moved to their present site in 1920, and in 1924 architects were commissioned to design a school and convent.

The design was executed in three construction phases between 1926 and 1950. The main structure is three stories in concrete block with a buff brick veneer covering. The east wing was built in 1926, the central section in 1936, and the north section and an extension of the central part in 1950.

The central pavilion exhibits a balconied portico, a stepped pediment and two-story arched windows. The change of window type on each floor is consistent with the style. Arched windows are found on the first story, straight-headed windows on the second and an enlarged belt course including frieze and cornice set off the smaller windows of the attic story. The distinctive clay tile roof was included to remind the sisters of their native home.

As community needs changed, and as the order became smaller, the school was closed in 1974. In the late 1990s, the sisters renovated part of the convent for the general community to use for low-income housing for the elderly.

The structure is very well maintained and is in excellent condition today.

3501 State St.
BUILT: 1926
ARCHITECT: *Matthew Lahr and Carl Strange*
STYLE: *Late Italian Renaissance Revival*

Designated Omaha Landmark: Oct. 17, 1978

Listed on the National Register of Historic Places

ENTIRELY ENCLOSED by the City National Bank Building, the interior elements create the grandeur of the Orpheum Theater. Originally built as the Creighton-Orpheum Theater in 1892, it opened as a live theater and vaudeville house with its main entrance located on 15th Street. In 1910, the City National Bank Building was constructed adjacent to the theater on the west side.

When the Creighton-Orpheum was badly damaged by a fire, it was replaced by a greatly expanded and reconfigured structure designed by the Chicago architects, Rapp and Rapp. The new three-story buff brick theater was incorporated into the City National Bank Building in 1927, at a cost of some $2 million. The new lobby and main entrance were reoriented to face 16th Street.

The largest of Omaha's theater "palaces," the three-level auditorium originally seated 2,877. The walls and ceilings are embossed with gold, silver and ivory patterns. Marble is used as the wainscotting and mirrors are alternated with panels of gold leaf, ivory and draperies. The focal point of the interior is a magnificent crystal chandelier, 16 feet in height, 9 feet in diameter, that weighs 4,500 pounds.

Closed in 1971, the Orpheum Theater was restored and renovated as a performing arts center and home for the Omaha Symphony in 1974. The theater now belongs to the City of Omaha, and is managed by a non-profit organization, the Omaha Performing Arts Society.

409 S. 16th St.
BUILT: 1927
ARCHITECT: *C. W. and George L. Rapp*
STYLE: *Second Renaissance Revival*

FATHER FLANAGAN RESIDENCE

Listed on the National Register of Historic Places

REV. EDWARD J. FLANAGAN, founded his refuge for homeless boys in Omaha in 1917 at 25th and Dodge Streets.

In October 1921, Flanagan relocated and established Boys Town as a separate municipality on the western edge of Omaha. His residence was constructed between 1926 and 1927. The design reflects the period revival-style that was popular at the time.

Constructed in brick, it exhibits a five-bay central block design, accented with a hipped roof, an open veranda on the east side, and two-story wings on both the west and south sides. Interior woodwork is oak.

In 1940, the house was extended to the west to provide dormitory housing for the De La Salle Christian Brothers. At the time, the main staircase was removed and placed opposite the south side entrance.

The house was restored in 1974 with a new staircase that was built in oak according to the original plans. The building has been arranged as a museum and the 1940 addition was converted into an alumni center.

Today, the Boys Town Hall of History welcomes visitors to this historic site.

Boys Town
BUILT: 1927
ARCHITECT: *Jacob M. Nachtigall*
STYLE: *Georgian Revival*

THIS HOUSE was one of the last large residential commissions undertaken by Thomas R. Kimball prior to his death in 1934. The home was created for William F. Baxter who was president of the Thomas Kilpatrick Co. and prominently associated with the development of Fontenelle Forest and the University of Omaha.

The house faces east and originally occupied a large lot on which Kimball also designed and planned the elaborate landscape and garden that no longer exists.

Constructed of concrete, masonry, and stucco over a steel framework, the house has a very pleasing open interior plan. With two full stories, the central exterior feature is a three-story tower. Originally, the house had a roof with green Spanish tile, which highlighted the exterior Spanish-style arches. A large open-air porch is located on the north side of the main level, and the south side features a two-level sun porch. Much use of

decorative limestone and terra cotta trim are Kimball touches for this Mediterranean design.

The garage was unusual for the time. It is accessed from the west side and located under the house making it one of the earliest homes in Omaha to have a "built-in" garage.

Interior features include decorative mosaic tile that was used on the entry hall floor and a circular stairway with wrought iron railing. The bedrooms on the second floor were situated along a corridor that runs the length of the house. This design arrangement, together with large casement windows, admits much air and light.

The house is now part of the campus of the University of Nebraska at Omaha and is used for the College of Social Services. Its future is uncertain.

410 S. Elmwood Blvd. (Road)
BUILT: 1927
ARCHITECT: *Thomas R. Kimball*
STYLE: *Eclectic/Mediterranean*

AMBASSADOR

LOCAL ARCHITECT James T. Allan, who practiced in Omaha from 1916 to 1945, designed these luxurious apartments in an exotic theme with Mediterranean influences.

arc 20 residential units. Exquisite detailing, fireplaces, and cathedral ceilings on the upper level, are some of the numerous distinctive interior features.

The structure is 120' x 87' and is three stories high with a raised parapet gable and balustrade at the roofline. The primary construction material is buff colored brick over a reinforced concrete frame. Variegated ceramic tile panels are set into the main façade, and there is extensive use of decorative terra cotta trim and ornamentation.

Contractor Alex Beck built the building for Joseph L. and Samuel N. Wolf. Total construction cost was $125,000 and there

The elegant main entrance is set within an artistic forecourt. Entrance pilasters topped with decorative lamps accent the courtyard entrance at the sidewalk. Sets of narrow, high arched windows add Mediterranean interest to the exterior.

For many years this apartment building has been owned and managed by the Novak Co. It is well maintained and adds much to the street scene.

111 S. 49th Ave.
BUILT: 1928
ARCHITECT: *James T. Allan*
STYLE: *Eclectic/Moorish–Mediterranean*

ON THE SOUTHWEST COR-NER of 14th and Farnam Streets, the magnificent Grand Central Hotel was built in 1873. After the Grand Central burned in 1878, the Kitchen brothers built the original Paxton Hotel in 1882 to replace it. The hotel was named for community leader and businessman William A. Paxton, one of the founders of the Omaha Stockyards and Paxton Vierling Steel Co.

In 1927, plans developed to create a new Paxton Hotel at the same location, and the old hotel was torn down. Architect Joseph G. McArthur of Omaha received the commission to design the new hotel in a more modern style. The new structure had 11 stories and was primarily of brick construction on a steel frame with reinforced concrete. Bedford limestone and terra cotta as used for exterior ornamentation. Described as fireproof, it measured 151′ x 132′.

The 325-room hotel was built by the Selden-Breck Co. at a cost of $1.5 million and opened the doors to receive guests June 26, 1929.

In the 1960s, operations as a hotel ceased. In July 1966, the structure was leased to the Federal Women's Job Corps as a residence for program participants until June 1969. Vacant for two years, it was taken over by an investment group, remodeled on the interior, and once again opened as a hotel in May 1971. Financial difficulties and a high vacancy rate caused the venture to fail.

Facing an uncertain future, the building was given a second reprieve when converted some years ago into an assisted living facility for the elderly and mentally disabled and called the Paxton Manor.

As the Paxton Manor closed in 2000, and has since been vacant, awaiting redevelopment plans. The hotel remains one of the few significant Art Deco structures in the city.

14th and Farnam Streets
BUILT: 1928
ARCHITECT: *Joseph G. McArthur*
STYLE: *Art Deco*

Designated Omaha Landmark: Sept. 9, 1980   *Listed on the National Register of Historic Places*

THIS OUTSTANDING EXAMPLE of Art Deco style and design is one of an important body of extant Art Deco structures in Omaha.

Constructed for $453,000, as a 12-story office tower, it is the first example in Omaha of a combination office structure and automobile parking facility. The name of the building recognizes the Redick family, prominent Omaha pioneers, who once owned the building site.

Built by the Parsons Construction Co. of Omaha, for Garrett and Agor, Inc., materials used in construction include reinforced concrete, brick and terra cotta. Aluminum panels appear above the entrance.

Rising to a height of 137 feet, the façade is emphasized by a series of three ziggurat setbacks. The vertical emphasis is further enhanced by the use of sunken panels of straight headed, steel casement windows. Hard-edged, low relief terra cotta panels are used as ornamentation.

Presently, the building is utilized as a hotel and is in very good condition.

1504 Harney St.
BUILT: 1930
ARCHITECT: *Joseph G. McArthur*
STYLE: *Art Deco*

AFTER THE DEATH of George A. Joslyn in 1916, his wife Sarah began to plan a suitable memorial for her husband. As he was deeply interested in art and music, she established the Society of Liberal Arts that would administer the museum and concert hall that eventually would be built.

Resembling an adaptation of an Egyptian temple, the Joslyn Memorial incorporated many Art Moderne motifs in its design. Constructed of pink Georgia marble, it is significant in both overall design and richness of material.

Mrs. Joslyn provided $2.6 million for its construction and a generous endowment for maintenance. Construction began Oct. 2, 1928, and was completed Nov. 29, 1931. A young architect,

Hershel Elarth, who was recommended by architect Thomas R. Kimball, assisted the McDonald firm and provided many of the innovative design features.

The structure included four large galleries, six small galleries, office space, a director's room, lecture hall and large concert hall, as well as a spacious central court with a skylight.

Due to a need for enlarged exhibit space, English architect Sir Norman Foster was commissioned to design an addition. Ground was broken for the addition on June 7, 1993, and the 58,000 square foot structure opened Nov. 19, 1994. The façade of the addition is pink Georgia marble, from the same quarry as the material for the original Joslyn Memorial.

2200 Dodge St.
BUILT: 1931
ARCHITECT: *John and Alan McDonald*
STYLE: *Art Moderne/Egyptian Revival*

Designated Omaha Landmark: Oct. 17, 1978   *Listed on the National Register of Historic Places*

THE OMAHA UNION STATION by Los Angeles architect, Gilbert Stanley Underwood, is an exceptional example of the Art Deco style. Built by Peter Kiewit and Sons of Omaha, it was completed in 1931 at a cost of $1,250,000. Faced with cream-colored, glazed terra cotta tile, the structure was built on a framework of structural steel, resting on concrete pilings.

Light colored pine and oak wood trim and black Belgian marble wainscotting were used with a terrazzo floor in the main waiting room. Belgium blue marble colonnades flank the 10 large, cathedral-style stained plate glass windows. Six 2,000-pound crystal and bronze chandeliers hang from the 60-foot ceiling.

At the grand opening of the station on Jan. 15, 1931, Gilbert Stanley Underwood, said, "We have tried to express the distinctive character of the railroad – strength, power and masculinity."

The station was closed May 1, 1971, with the end of the Union Pacific's passenger service. In 1973, Union Pacific Corporation donated the building to the City of Omaha. Today it is home to the Durham Western Heritage Museum.

10th and Marcy Streets
BUILT: 1931
ARCHITECT: *Gilbert Stanley Underwood*
STYLE: *Art Deco/Moderne*

THE SUPREME FOREST WOODMEN CIRCLE, the Woman's auxiliary of the Woodmen of the World fraternal insurance company, was organized in Omaha in 1894. Upon its founding, the group occupied office space with the Woodmen organization in the Sheely Block at 15th and Howard Streets.

When Woodmen of the World relocated in 1932 to more spacious offices in the Insurance Building at 17th and Farnam Streets, they again offered space to the Woodmen Circle. The Circle, determined to establish a more visible identity, made plans to construct a headquarters building at 33rd and Farnam Streets. The noted Omaha architect George B. Prinz was selected for the job.

Opened in January 1933, and dedicated in June of that year, the building is an elegant three-story structure. Constructed with a steel frame, it is entirely faced with Bedford limestone. The stone, an unusual pinkish buff color, was obtained from a quarry at Kasota, Minnesota. The design is "U" shape with two wings. There is a full basement and the entire building is fireproof.

When the building opened, it was considered to have one of the most elegant office interiors in Omaha.

The Woodmen Circle merged with the Woodmen of the World Jan. 1, 1965. This structure was later sold to Mutual of Omaha and incorporated into their complex of buildings.

3303 Farnam St.
BUILT: 1933
ARCHITECT: *George B. Prinz*
STYLE: *Georgian Revival*

IN 1930, the U.S. Government announced its intention to construct a new Federal Building in Omaha that would occupy the site of the old Army Building at 15th and Dodge Streets.

Plans for an 11-story modern design were unveiled in February 1932. The exterior featured the use of limestone and granite on the lower three floors, with the upper stories clad in brick.

Described as fireproof, the building has a steel frame encased in concrete, with reinforced concrete floors. In November 1932, a building permit was issued to the general contractor, J. P. Cullen and Sons, Inc., of Janesville, Wisconsin, and construction began.

The dedication on Feb. 27, 1934, commended the building "to honesty, higher efficiency and greater service." Special appreciation was expressed to the architects and contractors for making it possible to erect the building at a much lower cost than expected.

The Omaha Federal Office Building is a significant example of transitional design from classical revival to Moderne, and includes many Art Deco features. It is also representative of the ideals of public works projects undertaken during the Hoover and Roosevelt administrations.

106 S. 15th St.
BUILT: 1933
ARCHITECT: *Kimball, Steele and Sandham/George B. Prinz*
STYLE: *Art Deco/Moderne*

ORGANIZED IN OMAHA as the Municipal University in 1908, the first campus was located in north central Omaha. With increased enrollment, it became evident that a new site was needed, which would allow for expansion and development.

In the 1930s, with the advent of the Public Works Administration (PWA), Omaha University became aware of new possibilities.

The university decided to move forward (not without controversy) to identify a more suitable site. In the fall of 1936, a 20-acre tract of land on west Dodge Street was purchased from John P. Webster for $48,000. Because this land was outside the city limits, it first had to be annexed before the PWA grant could be approved. This accomplished, funds were granted and construction began in January 1937.

The Latenser firm provided the design for an enlarged Georgian Colonial Revival style building. It was constructed with brick veneer over a frame of steel and reinforced concrete. Work

progressed, and a cornerstone laying ceremony occurred in September 1937, with formal dedication of the building in November 1938.

At three and one-half stories, the building presents a classical façade, with a symmetrical wing at each end. The dominant feature is an elevated entry with pediment, supported by four large columns. A lantern cupola surmounts the moderately pitched roof.

When completed, the building included a lecture hall seating 300, a large auditorium for 1,000, 50 classrooms, and space for a 40,000-volume library. The facility was fully air-conditioned, distinguishing it as the only completely air-conditioned campus in the nation. The cost of the structure with landscaping was approximately $1 million when completed.

First named the Administration Building, it continues to serve the university as Arts and Science Hall.

60th and Dodge Streets
BUILT: 1938
ARCHITECT: *John Latenser and Sons*
STYLE: *Georgian Colonial Revival*

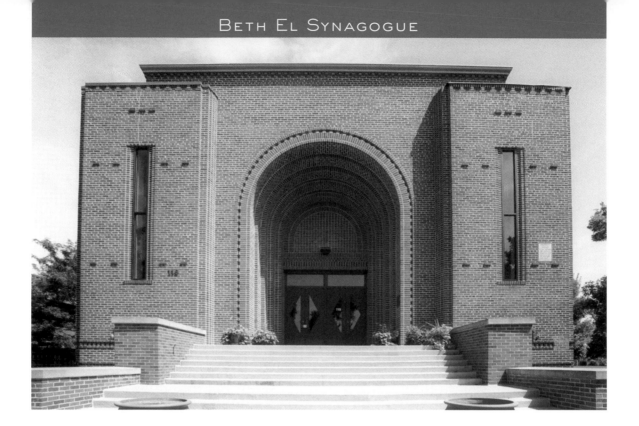

THIS STRUCTURE was originally built for the Beth El congregation. First organized in September 1929, the building site was purchased, and fund raising began in 1935. The synagogue was completed for dedication on Hanukkah in 1941.

Constructed of red brick over concrete, the central feature of the exterior is the massive rounded-arch entry in the west façade. The exterior walls exhibit tall, deeply set vertical windows, and a large flight of steps lead upward toward the entry. The interior contains 30,000 square feet and originally provided two large open assembly areas, apartments, offices, meeting rooms, and a kitchen. In 1952, Omaha architect Noel Wallace designed a large educational wing, which was built on the north side.

The Beth El congregation moved from the building in 1988. In 1991, Opera Omaha purchased the building. When this organization was unable to raise sufficient funds for re-development they offered it for sale in June 1994. At the time it was sold, a plan was afoot to demolish it and build apartment units on the site.

However, in September 1995, the firm of Holland Basham Architects purchased it, and with a complete renovation, converted it into offices for the firm. The original integrity of the exterior design is well preserved and the building is an outstanding example of historic preservation and adaptive reuse in Omaha.

210 S. 49th St.
BUILT: 1940
ARCHITECT: *John and Alan McDonald*
STYLE: *Mediterranean Revival*

By the end of World War II, the Omaha World-Herald newspaper offices at 15th and Farnam Streets were deemed inadequate. Plans were developed for construction of a new building that would be located on a city block bounded by Dodge Street to Capitol Avenue, and 13th to 14th Streets.

The Leo A. Daly Co. created a modern forward-looking design for a two-story structure with full basement that could easily be expanded. To accommodate the great weight of the equipment that would be installed, 130 concrete piers were sunk 50 feet to bedrock to create a foundation for the building. Excavation at the site began in September 1946.

On July 3, 1947, work had progressed and a ceremony was held to lay the cornerstone. By June 1948, basic construction was completed, and the Omaha World-Herald officially moved into their new home.

The new building was formed from a cast, reinforced concrete superstructure that was entirely faced with buff-pink Kasota limestone. Given the name World-Herald Square upon its completion, 1952 saw a major addition to the building which increased space by 50 percent. Other additions were made in 1954 and 1956. The structure continues to serve the newspaper today.

14th and Dodge Streets
BUILT: 1948
ARCHITECT: *Leo A. Daly Co.*
STYLE: *Modern*

In Omaha, it is now interesting to think of not only what happened in the last century but in the century before that, dramatizing the depth of our history as we move into the new century. And as we do so, it is increasingly important to balance the best of our historic past with our new development.

This balancing need not stand in the way of "progress" and if properly incorporated and designed, the blend of the old and the new makes each more dynamic. St. Mary Magdalene Church, on the site of new Roman L. Hruska Federal Courthouse in downtown Omaha, is a prime example of this. This alloy of an historic church and contemporary courthouse, in a glance, says a great deal about our city by illustrating a full spectrum of our character, with each enhancing the other.

So this book is not about preservation, it's about continuation — a continuation of our historic resources as contributors to our urban environment. Historic properties embody the best of our invested energy, and culture, and need only varying degrees of care to continue in productive use. This is not just for their architectural qualities but, from a conservation criteria, simply to be good stewards of our resources, both natural and cultural.

The stark fact is that when we lose an historic resource it is gone forever. There is no recreating it and no way to mitigate the damage. Demolition is forever and with every misdirected wrecking ball we irrevocably diminish our city's soul. This is a black and white issue; a building is either saved or lost, there is no compromise.

Taking stock of Omaha's architectural retention is a bleak endeavor. On the positive side we have saved some significant resources including the entire Old Market Area and such individual structures as the Omaha Building, Aquila Court, the Durham Western Heritage Museum and many others. On the downside, we have lost too many buildings and districts that would enrich our city if we had them today, most notably the old Post Office at 16th and Dodge Streets and the Jobbers Canyon Historic District. Out of the hundred plus buildings featured in Landmark's 1977 book, *Omaha City Architecture*, only some 70 survive today.

But buildings should not be saved just because they are old. Age is not the critical factor by itself. Architectural quality is the criteria. We would stand aside while an ungainly and crude historic building is demolished to make way for an attractive new one but, unfortunately, this is seldom the case. The buildings we advocate saving are well crafted and designed; positive contributors to our visual environment. These are objects of quality and what replaces them are often parking lots or buildings that rate aesthetically well below their predecessors. In the delicate makeup of our visual tapestry we can ill afford to lose a good building or build a bad one. So one easy and positive step for our urban quality is simply to keep the best of what we already have.

One of Omaha's strengths is our necklace of historic, inner city, neighborhoods. Positive strides have been taken in the care of these districts with strong neighborhood organizations such as the Field Club and Dundee-Memorial Park Associations that are critically important in maintaining their integrity. What Omaha needs now, more than ever, is to transfer this sensitivity to our most symbolic and visible neighborhood, our Downtown environs.

Omaha has long struggled to define who we are and what our image is, or should be. Omaha's authentic image is that of an historic river town and we should accept this mantle with pride and grace, building on our own uniqueness rather than trying to re-create ourselves as a northern Phoenix all new, shining and artificial. Our historic resources give us authenticity and substance, continuity and character — and authenticity is a fundamental requirement for any city to be noted and remembered.

We must continually take stock of these resources, evaluating who we are and what we want to be as a city — respecting our heritage as caretakers of our future.

GEORGE HAECKER, AIA
Past President, Landmarks, Inc.

Looking Northwest from the 10th Street Bridge

Standing (L to R): Unknown, Noel Wallace, 2 Unknowns, William Steele, Horrace Seymour, J. Dow Sandham, Unknown, Alan McDonald
Sitting Far Right is Thomas R. Kimball

FREDERICK A. HENNINGER (1865-1944)

Frederick A. Henninger, was an early Omaha architect who helped shape the commercial, industrial and residential areas of the community for half a century.

Henninger was born on a farm near Alba, Iowa, in 1865. He attended the Chicago Art Institute and was described as a "natural born artist." After two years of schooling he moved to Lincoln, Nebraska, where a local architect employed him. About 1891 he relocated to Omaha and worked as a laborer in the Union Pacific shops. In 1895 he began work as a draftsman for the firm of F.C. Ledebrink, and in the following year he purchased the business.

In 1898 Henninger was asked to design the Dairy Building for Omaha's Trans-Mississippi Exposition. He was soon designing major downtown office buildings as well as residences for many of the city's prominent citizens.

Major office and commercial buildings designed by Henninger include: the Securities Building, 16th and Farnam Streets; U.S. National Bank Building, 16th and Farnam Streets; Grain Exchange, 19th and Harney Streets; Farm Credit Building, 19th and Douglas Streets; and the Elmwood Park Pavilion.

Henninger designed residences for: Edgar Morsman, 518 S. 38th St.; O.H. Barmettler, 622 N. 38th St.; Fred Metz Jr., 115 N. 53rd St.; Lyman Perley, 207 Fairacres Rd.; and many others. He became recognized for his quickness and due to prolific output was known during his most active period as "house-a-day

Henninger." One hallmark of Henninger's design was his great attention to detail. Henninger's residences often had curved arches over a door or a window, and design details on the front usually carried through to all other sides.

Many buildings design by Henninger are listed on the National Register of Historic Places and five of Henninger's homes have been Omaha Symphony Showhouses. He retired in 1937 and moved to Pasadena, California, where he died in 1944.

THOMAS R. KIMBALL (1862–1934)

Thomas R. Kimball, a Nebraska architect with a considerable national reputation, was one of the Eclectic Era's most gifted. Educated at the University of Nebraska, then Cowles School of Art and the Massachusetts Institute of Technology in Boston, Kimball furthered his training in both art and architecture at the Ecolé Des Beaux Arts in Paris.

Together with C. Howard Walker, Kimball opened architectural offices in Boston, followed by an Omaha office in 1891. Walker and Kimball were appointed architects-in-chief for the Trans-Mississippi and International Exposition of 1898, which garnered wide praise from peers and received great national attention for its success. The partnership was disbanded following the Exposition, but then briefly reconstituted for work on the St. Louis World's Fair of 1904. Kimball maintained an office in Omaha as a sole proprietor until 1928, when the partnership of Kimball, Steele and Sandham was formed.

Throughout Kimball's long career, 871 commissions in all, this master of many architectural styles was the consummate advocate of quality in result and professionalism in the exercise. President Theodore Roosevelt appointed him to the first National Fine Arts Commission in 1909 and his peers and colleagues elected him president of the American Institute of Architects twice (1918-1920).

By appointment, Kimball acted as professional advisor to the Nebraska State Capitol Commission (1919-1932) and drew the rules of competition, which resulted in the selection of Bertram G. Goodhue as the architect of the capitol. He acted in similar capacity for the Kansas City Liberty War Memorial in 1920.

Kimball is remembered for notable designs in Omaha that include such residential structures as: the Chateausque Gurdon Wattles home, 320 S. 37th St.; the Italian Renaissance Kirkendall home, 3727 Jackson St.; and Kimball's mother's home at 2236 St. Mary's Ave. Commercial structures of note and memory include the Fontenelle Hotel, the old Burlington Station, and the old Omaha Public Library now known as the Historic Library Plaza.

Ecclesiastical architectural accomplishments include All Saints Episcopal Church and Parish House and the Spanish Renaissance Revival Saint Philomena's (Saint Francis Cabrini) Church and Rectory. Kimball's magnum opus, also in Spanish Renaissance form, is the monumental St. Cecilia's Cathedral, which is among the 10 largest Roman Catholic cathedrals in the United States.

Kimball passed away in Omaha in 1934.

JOHN LATENSER SR. (1858–1936)

John Latenser's architectural career spanned a half-century in Omaha. Born in Liechtenstein in 1858 and trained in architecture at the Polytechnic College in Stuttgart, Germany, Latenser arrived in Chicago at age 21 to accept a position as a draftsman. He remained there for several years prior to settling in Omaha and securing employment with F.M. Ellis. There he drew the plans for the old Brownell Hall on South 10th Street.

In 1886 Latenser established his own practice with offices in the Merchants National Bank building. Upon winning an architectural competition for the design of Webster School he embarked upon a long career that included designs for Bancroft, Castelar, Miller Park, Dundee, Cass, Pacific and Saunders Schools.

Commissions for many of the city's public and commercial buildings produced such structures as Central High School, the Douglas County Courthouse and the J.L. Brandeis and Sons store. Additionally, Latenser was appointed by the McKinley Administration to the position of Superintendent of Public Buildings for the Central Western States District, with offices in Omaha.

John Latenser was a student of art, history, literature and music. With a fondness for opera and classical music, he spoke fluent German, French, Swiss and Italian.

Latenser's sons, John Jr. and Frank, joined him in practice in later years and the firm became John Latenser and Sons. He died in Omaha in 1936 at the age of 78.

From left, John Jr., John Sr. and Frank Latenser at John Latenser & Sons architecture firm at 1307 Farnam St.

JOHN MCDONALD (1861-1956)

The architectural practice of John McDonald and his son Alan embraced three quarters of a century. A native of Canada, the senior McDonald received his architects training at McGill University in Montreal. He came to America in the 1880s and eventually settled in Omaha.

With David Olgilvy, a college classmate, McDonald established a practice in 1887 as McDonald and Ogilvy. In 1890 Olgilvy left Omaha and the firm thereafter operated in McDonald's name. John McDonald developed his successful practice through residential commissions from numerous of Omaha's wealthy and prominent business leaders.

The earliest of McDonald's important creations is the Scottish Baronial home of George and Sarah Joslyn, 3902 Davenport St. The 35-room mansion situated on five and one-half acres features turrets topped by battlements, crenellated porches and gabled dormers.

After receiving an architectural degree from Harvard College in 1915, Alan McDonald (1891-1947) joined the senior McDonald's practice the following year. Together, the father-son team assumed a major role in developing the architectural landscape of Omaha for the next 30 years.

Jointly, the McDonalds produced the city's finest example of Georgian Colonial Revival architecture in their composition of the First Unitarian Church, 3114 Harney St. This purest example of the style is constructed in red brick with projecting front portico and a three-section bell tower.

In the succeeding years, the McDonalds were identified with both the Prairie School Design (which Alan McDonald called Prairie Architecture) and a shift toward Art Deco and Moderne. The latter form received much attention as the result of Bertram G. Goodhue's acclaimed design of the Nebraska State Capitol in 1919.

As Sarah Joslyn planned a memorial to her husband, the McDonald's adapted their design to reflect the concept of modern expression in the Joslyn Art Museum, 22nd and Dodge Streets. Other important examples of the McDonald's work include the Bradford-Pettis house, Charles D. McLaughlin house, Beth El Synagogue and the Hill Hotel.

Alan McDonald preceded his father in death, passing away in 1947. John McDonald died in 1956 at the age of 95.

MENDELSSOHN, FISHER AND LAWRIE

GEORGE FISHER (1856-1931)

The firm of Mendelssohn, Fisher and Lawrie evolved from one of the city's earliest professional partnerships - Dufrene and Mendelssohn, formed in 1881. Dufrene had worked as an architect in Nebraska since 1867,

HARRY LAWRIE (ca. 1838-1935)

first in partnership with T. B. Borst, and then alone during the 1870's. Mendelssohn, born in Berlin in 1842, had studied in New York and practiced in Detroit prior to coming to Omaha. The 1884 Christian Specht Building is a product of the Dufrene and Mendelssohn partnership.

In 1885 Mendelssohn left Dufrene and entered into partnership with George Fisher. The firm operated as Mendelssohn and Fisher in 1885 and 1886 and then as Mendelssohn and Lawrie in 1887 when Fisher left the firm for a year and Harry Lawrie joined Mendelssohn. Fisher then rejoined the firm and the partnership of Mendelssohn, Fisher and Lawrie was formed.

Mendelssohn, Fisher and Lawrie was a prestigious firm which designed a variety of prominent buildings in Omaha's building boom of the 1880s and early 1890s. Mendelssohn left in 1893, and the partnership of Fisher and Lawrie continued until 1913. The partners were agile designers working in a variety of building types and styles. Their existing buildings include the Old University Library (Lincoln), the Gottlieb Storz House and Sacred Heart Church.

Michigan-born George Fisher graduated from the University of Michigan in 1880 with a degree in civil engineering. Harry Lawrie had nine years of professional experience in Glasgow and Edinburgh, Scotland, before immigrating to Chicago in 1883 to enter the office of Burham and Root. He moved to Omaha in 1887. Lawrie's last commission was the design for the old municipal airport in 1935.

GEORGE B. PRINZE (1864-1946)

Architect George B. Prinze arrived in Omaha in 1891 to assume the position of chief draftsman in the office of Thomas R. Kimball. A talented artist, Prinz was educated at the Massachusetts Institute of Technology and spent two years in additional study in Europe before taking his first position in the office of architect J. William Beal in Boston.

Prinz established his own practice in 1909, and was a member of the Omaha City Planning Commission from its inception in 1916 until his retirement in 1939. His buildings during a long career represented some of the finest residences, churches and commercial structures in the city and demonstrated a range of forms to include Renaissance Revival, Eclectic and Art Deco to Moderne.

Especially significant creations were the residences of Charles Metz, 3708 Dewey Ave, and that of Lewis C. Nash, 3708 Burt St. Important commercial buildings include the Flatiron Hotel, the Livestock Exchange Building, and the Masonic Temple at 19th and Douglas Streets. Prinz's collegiate Gothic First Presbyterian Church has been described as on of Omaha's finest.

In later years, George Prinz completed the Woodmen Circle Building in a pleasing amalgam of Art Deco and Moderne styles and also collaborated in an association with the firm of Kimball, Steele and Sandham in the execution of the Art Deco Federal Building at 15th and Dodge Streets.

Prinz devoted time throughout his life developing an interest and apparent natural talent to painting in watercolor medium. His home on South Elmwood Boulevard included one of the finest and most extensive private collections of books on art and architectural subjects in the area. Prinz passed away in 1946 at the age of 42.

Clockwise from top left: Mary Rogers Kimball Residence, William F. Baxter Residence, Mary Rogers Kimball Residence, Beals Elementary

ANTEFIXES (ANTEFIXA)

Decorative marble or terra cotta blocks used to hide the ends of the tiles on the lower sections of classical buildings.

ARCH

A structure built over an opening, designed to transform the downward pressure into lateral thrust. Arches come in many different shapes and styles.

ART NOUVEAU

A style of architecture and interior decor dating from the late 1800s marked by the use of undulation, such as waves, flames, flower stalks and flowing hair.

ART DECO

A term derived from the 1925 Paris Exposition Internationale des Arts Decoratifs et Industriels Modernes, now loosely applied to design of the late 1920s and 1930s. Basically a style of sumptuous surface decoration which relies heavily on rectilinear forms, geometricized curves, chevrons and zig-zags. Also characterized by crystalline, faceted forms.

ATRIUM

An inner courtyard that is open to the sky or covered by a skylight.

BALUSTER

A short post or pillar in a series that supports a rail, thus forming a balustrade.

BARREL TILES

Rounded clay roof tiles most often used on Spanish-style houses.

BEAD MOLDING

A small, cylindrical molding enriched with ornaments resembling a string of beads.

BEAUX-ARTS CLASSICISM

A style of architecture and ornamentation that flourished in turn-of-the-century America. Named after the leading school of architecture of the period, the Ecole des Beaux-Arts, in Paris, the style employs strict symmetry in composition, free combinations of elements of classical architecture and the use of coupled columns, monumental flights of steps and figurative sculpture.

BRACKET

A supporting piece of wood or stone, often formed of scrolls or other decorative shapes, designed to bear a projected weight, such as a window.

CAPITAL

The head or crowning feature of a column.

CASTELLATED

Decorated with battlements (a parapet with alternating indentations and raised portions); also called crenellation. Buildings with battlements are usually brick or stone.

CHATEAUESQUE

A late 19th century style of American architecture combining elements of Late French Gothic and French Renaissance architecture, characterized by masonry construction, asymmetrical plans and silhouettes, steep-hipped roofs surmounted by metal railings, round turrets with "candle-snuffer" roofs and wall dormers.

CLAPBOARD

Overlapping horizontal boards that cover the timber-framed wall of a house.

CLERESTORY WINDOW

A window placed in the upper walls of a room to provide extra light.

COLLIGATE GOTHIC

A style of turn-of-the-century American architecture inspired by Gothic architecture and frequently found on college campuses. Also known as Late Gothic Revival, this style is characterized by masonry construction and a reliance on forms from the English Perpendicular Gothic.

CORINTHIAN

A classical Greek architectural order whose column has an ornate capital using stylized acanthus leaves.

CORNICE

Any projecting ornamental molding that finishes or crowns the top of a building, wall, arch, etc.

CUPOLA

A dome on a circular or polygonal base crowning a roof or turret.

DOME

An arched roof or ceiling of even curvature erected on a circular or square base. Domes can be segmented, semicircular, pointed or bulbous.

DORIC

A classical Greek architectural order whose column has only a simple decoration around the top, and a fluted shaft.

DORMER WINDOW

A window placed vertically in a sloping roof that has a small roof of its own. Most often seen in second-floor bedrooms.

EASTLAKE

Named for British designer Charles Eastlake, the style stressed lighter, geometric forms of decoration in contrast to the curved designs of earlier Victorian style. Rectilinear and adorned with incised designs it stressed mutual respect and harmony between function and beauty.

EAVES

The lower part of a roof projecting beyond the face of a wall.

ENGLISH PERPENDICULAR

The last phase of English Gothic architecture characterized by tracery in which the pattern is formed by multiplying the mullions in the upper part of the window and by a general tendency to stress vertical moldings.

FACING

A covering applied to the outer surface of a building.

FANLIGHT

A window, often semicircular, with radiating glazing bars suggesting a fan that is placed over a door.

FASCIA

A horizontal piece (such as a board) covering the joint between the top of a wall and the projecting eaves; also called a fascia board.

FIELDSTONE

Rough, irregularly shaped pieces of rock that can be used to cover the surface of a building, make a walkway, line a garden bed, etc.

FINIAL

A formal ornament at the top of a canopy, gable, pinnacle, etc.

FLUTING

Shallow, concave grooves running vertically on the shaft of a column, pilaster or other surface.

FOYER

The entrance hall of a building.

FRIEZE

A decorated band along the upper part of a wall.

GABLE

The triangular upper portion of a wall at the end of a pitched roof.

GAMBREL ROOF

A roof with one low, steep slope and an upper, less-steep one on each of its two sides, giving the look of a traditional American hay barn.

GARGOYLE

A figurine that projects from a roof or the parapet of a wall or tower and is carved into a grotesque figure, human or animal.

GEORGIAN STYLE

A turn-of-the-century American architecture style that referred back to English and colonial architecture of the mid-seventeenth century, the rule of George III. When drawing directly on colonial sources, Georgian Revival tends to be rectangular in plan, symmetrical in composition, with classical detailing; the central part of the façade is usually projecting, pedimental or has a portico.

GREEK REVIVAL

An early nineteenth century American architectural style which relied on the simple classical elements of Greek architecture; among them bilateral symmetry, simple rectangular shapes placed together, smooth wall surfaces, low roof pitch, lack of ornamentation and white surfaces.

HALF-TIMBERING

A method of construction featuring walls built of timber framework with the spaces filled in by plaster or brickwork.

HIPPED ROOF

A roof that slopes inward on all sides.

IONIC

A classical Greek architectural order whose distinctive column capital is composed of volutes.

Italianate

A mid-nineteenth century American architectural style which modeled itself after the Italian villa. A square or octagonal tower is the most common feature; other include smooth wall surfaces, roof eaves supported by brackets, round-headed and bay windows, balconies, verandas, loggias and an overall scheme of well-defined rectilinear blocks grouped in an asymmetrical manner.

Jacobethan Revival

A turn-of-the-century American architectural style combining elements of English architecture from the time of Elizabeth I and James I. Characteristics: stone and brick rectangular windows divided by stone mullions into rectangular sections, steep-sided triangular gables or gables composed of segmented curves and straight line in combination, tall chimneys and round-arched doorways.

Lancet

A sharp pointed arch.

Lattice window

A window with diamond-shaped leaded lights or glazing bars arranged like an openwork screen; also, loosely, any hinged window, as distinct from a sash window.

Lintel

A horizontal beam or stone bridging an opening.

Mansard roof

This roof is flat on top, sloping steeply down on all four sides, thus appearing to sheath the entire top story of a house or other building.

Mullion

A vertical member dividing windows into two or more lights.

National Register of Historic Places

The National Register of Historic Places is the nation's official list of cultural resources worthy of preservation. Authorized under the National Historic Preservation Act of 1966, the National Register is part of a national program to coordinate and support public and private efforts to identify, evaluate, and protect historic and archeological resources. Properties listed in the Register include districts, sites, buildings, structures, and objects that are significant in American history, architecture, archeology, engineering, and culture. The National Register is administered by the National Park Service, which is part of the U.S. Department of the Interior. For more information visit www.nationaltrust.org.

Nave

The main body of a church flanked by aisles.

Neoclassical

The European style of architecture prominent from the late eighteenth century until the mid-nineteenth century, distinguished from its predecessor, the Baroque style, by greater simplicity and a more reverent imitation of ancient classical models, particularly Greek forms.

Niche

A recess in a wall to hold a statue or object. Usually curved at the back.

Omaha Landmark

The nine-member Omaha Landmarks Heritage Preservation Commission was created by a city ordinance in 1977 to designate structures and districts of local significance. Omaha Landmark properties must be historically or architecturally significant. The commission regulates work done on designated buildings and identifies and implements the overall goals and objectives for preservation in Omaha. For more information visit www.ci.omaha.ne.us/landmarks/default.htm.

Palladian window

A triple opening, the central one arched and wider than the others which are square topped.

Parapet

The portion of a wall extending above the roof.

Pedestal

The supporting parts of a column or colonnade.

Pediment

A low-pitched triangular gable above a portico or a doorway.

Pilaster

A shallow pier or a rectangular column projecting only slightly from a wall.

Portico

A colonnaded porch.

Porte-cochere

A roofed structure extending over an adjacent driveway to shelter those getting in or out of vehicles.

Prairie School

An early twentieth century American architectural style originated by Frank Lloyd Wright's attempts to unite structure with landscape. The style emphasizes the horizontal as seen in horizontal bands of windows, low roofs and accentuated horizontal structural and ornamental elements.

Queen Anne Style

A mid-nineteenth century style of architecture that borrowed elements originating in England at the time of Queen Anne; irregularity of play and massing, variety in colors and textures, bay windows, high and multiple roofs, large gables, large chimneys and small scale classic detail.

Quoins

The dressed stones at the corners of buildings, usually laid so their faces are alternately large and small. Usually in contrasting color of brick from the rest of the wall. Common accent in Georgian homes.

Renaissance Revival

A mid-nineteenth century style of architecture that borrowed heavily from the forms developed in the Italian Renaissance; simple straight-fronted buildings with heavy projecting cornices, symmetrical composition, rusticated ground floors, smooth and plain wall surfaces and balustraded balconies.

Richardsonian Romanesque

A late nineteenth century American architectural style based upon American architect H. H. Richardson's personal re-interpretation of Romanesque architecture. Massiveness and weight are its chief characteristics.

Rustication

Masonry cut in massive blocks separated by deep joints, used to give a rich, bold texture to an outside wall.

Sash window

A window formed with sashes, or sliding frames running in vertical grooves.

Soffit

The underside of any architectural element (as of an overhang or staircase).

Solarium

A glass-enclosed porch or room, often used to display flowers and other plants; also called a sunroom or garden room.

Stanchion

A vertical steel support.

Stucco

A sturdy type of plaster used on exterior walls; often applied in a decorative pattern.

Terra cotta

Clay baked in moulds for use as roof tiles or building ornament.

Terrazzo

A sturdy flooring finish of marble chips mixed with cement mortar. After drying, the surface is ground and polished.

Transept

The area of a cross-shaped church intersecting with the nave at the crossing.

Transom

Small, usually rectangular or fanlight window over a door.

Tuscan

One of the five classical orders of architecture of Roman origin and plain in style.

Vergeboards

Projecting boards placed against the incline of the gable of a building and hiding the ends of the horizontal roof timbers; sometimes decorated.

Volutes

The scroll of an Ionic column.

Andreas, A.T. (ed.), *History of the State of Nebraska,* Chicago, The Western Historical Co., 1882. Reproduced in two volumes by the Nebraska State Historical Society, Lincoln, 1975.

Burkley, Frank J., *The Faded Frontier,* Burkley Envelope and Printing Co., Omaha, 1935.

Byron Reed Co., Inc., *The Story of Omaha,* Omaha, 1946.

A Comprehensive Program for Historic Preservation in Omaha, Landmarks Heritage Preservation Commission, Omaha, 1980.

Dustin, Dorothy D. *Omaha and Douglas County: A Panoramic History*, Windsor Publications, Woodland Hills, Calif., 1980.

An Inventory of Historic Omaha Buildings, Landmarks, Inc. and Landmarks Heritage Preservation Commission, Omaha, 1980.

McAlester, Virginia and Lee, *A Field Guide to America's Historic Neighborhoods and Museum Houses,* Alfred A. Knopf, New York, 1998.

Morearty, E.F., *Omaha Memories: Recollections of Events, Men and Affairs in Omaha, Nebraska from 1879 to 1917,* Swartz Printing Co., Omaha, 1917.

Omaha City Architecture, Landmarks, Inc. and the Junior League of Omaha, Inc., 1977.

Pen and Sunlight Sketches of Omaha and Environs, Phoenix Publishing Co., Chicago, 1892.

Savage, James W. and John T. Bell, *History of Omaha Nebraska and South Omaha*, Munsell and Co., New York, 1894.

Sorenson, Alfred, *History of Omaha from Pioneer Days to the Present Time*, Gibson, Miller and Richardson, Omaha, 1889.

Sorenson, Alfred, *Omaha Illustrated: A History of the Pioneer Period and the Omaha of Today*, Dunbar and Co., Omaha, 1888.

Sorenson, Alfred, *The Story of Omaha from Pioneer Days To the Present Time,* National Printing Co., Omaha, 1923.

Wakely, Arthur C. (ed.), *Omaha: The Gate City and Douglas County Nebraska: A Record of Settlement, Organization, Progress and Achievement,* Vol. 1 and 2, S.J. Clarke Co., Chicago, 1917.

Whiffen, Marcus *American Architecture Since 1780,* The M.I.T. Press, Cambridge, Mass., 1969.

Whithey, Henry F. and Elsie Rathburn, *Biographical Dictionary of American Architects (Deceased)*, New Age Publishing Co., Los Angeles, 1956.

Looking East from Capitol Avenue